THE KING OF TARS

MIDDLE ENGLISH TEXTS SERIES

GENERAL EDITOR
Russell A. Peck, University of Rochester

ASSOCIATE EDITOR
Alan Lupack, University of Rochester

ASSISTANT EDITOR
Pamela M. Yee, University of Rochester

ADVISORY BOARD

Theresa Coletti
University of Maryland

Rita Copeland
University of Pennsylvania

Susanna Fein
Kent State University

Thomas G. Hahn
University of Rochester

David A. Lawton
Washington University in St. Louis

Michael Livingston
The Citadel

R. A. Shoaf
University of Florida

Lynn Staley
Colgate University

Eve Salisbury
Western Michigan University

Bonnie Wheeler
Southern Methodist University

The Middle English Texts Series is designed for classroom use. Its goal is to make available to teachers, scholars, and students texts that occupy an important place in the literary and cultural canon but have not been readily available in student editions. The series does not include those authors, such as Chaucer, Langland, or Malory, whose English works are normally in print in good student editions. The focus is, instead, upon Middle English literature adjacent to those authors that teachers need in compiling the syllabuses they wish to teach. The editions maintain the linguistic integrity of the original work but within the parameters of modern reading conventions. The texts are printed in the modern alphabet and follow the practices of modern capitalization, word formation, and punctuation. Manuscript abbreviations are silently expanded, and *u/v* and *j/i* spellings are regularized according to modern orthography. Yogh (ȝ) is transcribed as *g, gh, y,* or *s,* according to the sound in Modern English spelling to which it corresponds; thorn (þ) and eth (ð) are transcribed as *th.* Distinction between the second person pronoun and the definite article is made by spelling the one *thee* and the other *the,* and final *-e* that receives full syllabic value is accented (e.g., *charité*). Hard words, difficult phrases, and unusual idioms are glossed either in the right margin or at the foot of the page. Explanatory and textual notes appear at the end of the text, often along with a glossary. The editions include short introductions on the history of the work, its merits and points of topical interest, and brief working bibliographies.

This series is published in association with the University of Rochester.

Medieval Institute Publications is a program of
The Medieval Institute, College of Arts and Sciences

 WESTERN MICHIGAN UNIVERSITY

THE KING OF TARS

Edited by

John H. Chandler

TEAMS • Middle English Texts Series

MEDIEVAL INSTITUTE PUBLICATIONS
Western Michigan University
Kalamazoo

Library of Congress Cataloging-in-Publication Data

King of Tars / edited by John H. Chandler.
    pages cm. -- (Middle English texts series)
 Text in Middle English; introduction and notes English.
 Includes bibliographical references.
  ISBN 978-1-58044-204-6 (paperbound : alk. paper)
 1. King of Tars. 2. Muslims--Poetry. 3. Kings and rulers--Poetry. 4. Conversion to Christi-
anity--Poetry. 5. Romances, English. I. Chandler, John H., 1974- editor.
 PR2065.K65 2015
 821'.1–dc23

                                                 2014043001

ISBN 978-1-58044-204-6

P 5 4 3 2 1

Printed and bound by CPI Group (UK) Ltd, Croydon, CR0 4YY

CONTENTS

Acknowledgments

I am grateful to the ongoing support of Thomas Hahn and Russell A. Peck for introducing me to this text and encouraging my pursuit of this edition, as well as for their sage guidance and friendship. Kristi J. Castleberry and Kara L. McShane, two colleagues and friends at the University of Rochester, read through this work and offered insightful advice and welcome enthusiasm. Alan Lupack read a later version and offered many improvements. The Middle English Texts Series would not be possible without generous support from the National Endowment of the Humanities. Martha M. Johnson-Olin and Pamela M. Yee prepared the volume for the press. My thanks also go to Patricia Hollahan, managing editor of Medieval Institute Publications, and her staff for expertly reading the text and bringing it to print. Finally, I am especially grateful to my wife, Francine, for her patience and support as I worked long hours and rambled on about medieval English culture, language, and textual habits in preparing this edition.

❧ INTRODUCTION

The King of Tars is a short poem whose purpose is to highlight and celebrate the power of Christianity. For centuries the poem's merits have slipped by outside the radar screen of medieval scholars because of its peculiar defiance of the usual categories of classification. It is neither a saint's life or a romance, nor a political drama or a miracle tale; rather it is a story inseminated by all of these genres. As a hagiographic work, its focus on temporal situations, especially political stability and inheritance, distracts the audience from the dream-vision and miracles on which the plot relies; as a romance, its focus on a female protagonist, rather than a male, seems oddly out of place. It is only when the various generic categories are layered together that the poem is best understood. Its role as entertainment is undeniable, but that entertainment thinly veils didactic intent. Many of the effects and plot developments — the transformations, namelessness of the principal characters, and exotic setting in the East — should be read through the lens of religious instruction. This early romance (c. 1330 or earlier) addresses religious interests through rhetorical trappings that parse, reinforce, educate, and entertain simultaneously.

THE PLOT

An early variant of the Constance tale, whose most famous English versions are told by Gower's Genius in the *Confessio Amantis* and Chaucer's Man of Law, *The King of Tars* carefully constructs its narrative to emphasize a broad array of ideas about race, gender, and religion. The Christian king of an eastern land named Tars has a beautiful wife and an even more beautiful daughter. The sultan of nearby Damas hears tales of the princess's beauty and demands her hand in marriage. The king of Tars refuses, as the sultan is not Christian, and a war ensues. The king of Tars quickly finds himself losing the war, and the princess offers to wed the sultan to end the bloodshed. After some convincing, the king and queen accede to her request, and the sultan takes the princess to Damas. Despite the princess's beauty, the sultan refuses to wed her until she converts to Islam. That night, the princess has a dream reassuring her that everything will turn out for the best if she does not stop believing in her heart in the power of Christianity. The princess pretends to convert and is wed to the sultan. She quickly becomes pregnant, and when the child is born, it is a formless lump of flesh. Recognizing the misshapen child as a sign of spiritual or religious conflict, the sultan rightly accuses the princess of false conversion, and she responds by proposing a test of faith. Each of the parents is to prove the power of his or her religion by praying that the lump-child be given form. The sultan places the lump on his altar and prays but to no avail. The princess asks that a priest be freed from the sultan's prison and bids him baptize the lump. Upon baptism, the lump-child gains human form, and the sultan recognizes the power of Christianity: he himself converts. When the sultan is baptized, the power of his new faith is

1

made apparent by a change of his skin from black to white. The sultan then joins forces with the king of Tars; he asks his people to convert to Christianity, and if they do not, he executes them. The poem ends with another battle, wherein the Christian sultan of Damas and king of Tars fight five Saracen kings. The Christians are victorious, and the principals, we are told, live a happy life and are accepted into Heaven.

GENRE

Stanley J. Solomon writes that "the problem of defining film genre does not seem very great until one reads the critics. Then what appears to be a genre to one writer becomes a subgenre to another, and what to one is merely a technique or a style becomes to another an identifiable manner of grouping."[1] Though Solomon was opening a discussion of film, his remark is equally applicable to medieval literature, especially Middle English romances, which tend to draw upon the conventions of multiple genres in order to pursue diverse objectives. Such is the case with *The King of Tars*, where the combination of hagiography, romance, and straightforward didacticism celebrate the power of Christianity. At the risk of sounding like Shakespeare's Polonius describing theatrical genre, when approaching *The King of Tars*, we are perpetually confronted by the pedantry of generic classification: is the poem a romantic hagiography or a hagiographical romance?[2]

In her discussion of romance, Susan Crane writes, "Genre was not an important concept for medieval theorists, nor did poets restrict the term *roman/romaunce* to one set of characteristics."[3] While there has been a recent surge of controversy in defining romance as a genre, the basic structure of a romance is largely agreed upon. One key feature is, as Alison Wiggins notes, that "romance involves a journey or quest of some kind. This may be an exile, banishment, separation, seeking of fortune, abduction, abandonment, or a crusade."[4] This quest is often resolved, at least in part, on the battlefield, and it is here that the romance and epic share common themes. However, while the epic is generally content to remain in the masculine world of *comitatus* and warfare, the romance is primarily interested in the private life of the hero, often in his love life or family relationships. As Ronald B. Herzman, Graham Drake, and Eve Salisbury observe, romances combine "the masculine, battlefield world of the *chanson de geste* with the increasing upper-class interest in what we would now call 'romantic love.'"[5] It is in that new focus on romantic love and family that two major threads of *The King of Tars* are spun: a new importance for women, especially the princess in relation to her father and her husband, combined with a greater emphasis on

---

[1] Solomon, *Beyond Formula*, p. 2.

[2] The reference to Shakespeare is, of course, where Polonius is speaking to Hamlet about the players. He praises them as "The best actors in the world, either for tragedy, / comedy, history, pastoral, pastoral-comical, his-/torical-pastoral, tragical-historical, tragical-comical-/historical-pastoral, scene individable, or poem un-/limited" (*Hamlet*, II.ii.392–96). Regardless of what they do, there must be a genre somewhere.

[3] Crane, *Insular Romance*, p. 10. Mehl argues, "The fact that [*The King of Tars*] is always classed with the romances again reveals how inadequate some of our definitions of medieval genre are" (*Middle English Romances*, p. 124).

[4] *Stanzaic Guy of Warwick*, ed. Wiggins, p. 8.

[5] Herzman, Drake, and Salisbury, eds., *Four Romances of England*, p. 2.

the personal journey and the individual's role in social and political events. The princess is the focus of the poem, in that it is her beauty that spurs the sultan to make war; she is the one to conceive of and implement a means to peace; she, not the sultan, correctly reads the monstrous birth; she is the driving force behind the conversion miracles, though she does not officiate in either baptism; and she brings about the happy ending through the challenges that face her. Though the poem opens and closes on the battlefield and is named for the king of Tars, his daughter's journey — both physical, as she travels to Damas, and religious, as she passes through a false conversion and leads the sultan of Damas to Christianity — perpetually marks the pulse of the poem.

Other romance components within the story include its verse form and repeated invocations of oral recitation. The poem is written in tail-rhyme, "an indigenous English verse form . . . used almost exclusively for romances."[6] Rhiannon Purdie has examined it in *Anglicising Romance: Tail-rhyme and Genre in Medieval English Literature*, where she notes that "tail-rhyme *romance* is, as far as we know, unique to Middle English."[7] She further notes that thirty-six poems, approximately one-third of the extant corpus of verse romances, are wholly or partially written in tail-rhyme stanzas.[8] Most of these, including *The King of Tars*, are early compositions. The signature form of tail-rhyme stanzas is a rhyme scheme of *aabccbddbeeb* or the more demanding *aabaabccbddb* formula used by *The King of Tars*. Such a scheme readily adapted to written vernacular romances, and it would certainly have been helpful as an aid to memory, both for the raconteur and the audience at an oral presentation.

One recurrent feature of *The King of Tars* is the invocation characteristic of minstrelsy, an oral technique invoking memory that reaches as far back as Homer and the epic tradition. Though earlier scholars argued "that the romances were composed by minstrels, or by others writing for minstrel performance," Harriet Hudson suggests that the invocation of oral narration in Middle English romances may be mainly "a nostalgic feature of genre validation."[9] The current poem certainly uses these rhetorical features to engage an audience accustomed to listening to an oral recitation, though the fact that the earliest witness, the Auchinleck manuscript, is not the original version of the narrative further supports the earlier scholars' theory that, in some cases at least, the written texts were the result of recitation that was simply committed to writing. While oral performance is not limited to romances — homilies, for example, were mainly written to be heard, rather than read — the frequency with which romances invoke tropes of oral or minstrel presentation is striking and from the outset is a common feature of the genre. It is absolutely one on which the current poem draws, given its early date.

In all these respects it is fairly clear that *The King of Tars* fits comfortably into the general parameters of the romance. Its formal features — including the tail-rhyme and reliance on oral recitation tropes, as well as its motifs including romantic love, family expectations, and its focus on social and political concerns — suggest that genre. However, romances almost always feature strong, martial male protagonists; though such a hero is suggested by the title, the eponymous king of the poem is, in fact, a marginal character,

---

[6] Hudson, ed., *Four Middle English Romances*, p. 2.

[7] Purdie, *Anglicising Romance*, p. 1.

[8] Purdie, *Anglicising Romance*, p. 1.

[9] Hudson, ed., *Four Middle English Romances*, p. 2.

important for the framing battles, but not present for the bulk of the narrative. Instead, the principal protagonist is his daughter.[10] There is no knightly adventure, and though the physical journey of the princess and, to a certain extent, the spiritual journey of the sultan take center stage, neither journey defines the focus of the whole narrative. Travel adventure heroines often have to go outside their home, religion, and culture, and adapt as circumstances require. This trope is at the heart of the Constance story and its analogues, where the heroine survives within a hostile pagan world.

Though Tars's daughter is the central figure of the poem, her agency is quite different from that of a knight in a typical romance. While most romances linger on social concerns, especially the establishment of the protagonist within society, *The King of Tars* is too interested in spiritual concerns, mainly defined by the woman, that culminate in a mass conversion, to be categorized solely as a typical travel romance narrative.

Given its multiple settings, particularly the juxtaposition of the Saracen and Christian worlds, it fits well enough into the most characteristic of romance travel narratives, the *chanson d'aventure*. As I have noted, *Tars* ties in somewhat with the Constance tales, in that an emperor's daughter leaves her home culture to be married to a sultan, though the differences between *Tars* and the Constance tales are considerably greater than the likenesses. In *Tars* there are no hints of the woman's fleeing her father for fear of incest, as there are in early versions of the story and in the Middle English romance *Emaré*, nor are there any affiliations with the most central feature of the Constance stories, namely, the calumniated queen motif. In *Tars* the sultan's bride seems to be the model of the good queen until it is made apparent that she has not been strictly obedient to the sultan's demands. One result of her disobedience is that she does give birth to a monster, such as Donegild invented in Chaucer's Man of Law's Tale, though not for reasons of adultery but rather for Christian fidelity. There are no wicked mothers-in-law, only the sultan himself to charge her, and she readily acknowledges the charge of breach of faith with the Saracen idols. By asking her husband to put their respective gods to the test, which he agrees to do, she ultimately acts according to their mutual benefit, as she watches over their general welfare.

This brings up another crucial difference between *Tars* and other Constance tales. In Trevet, the Emperor's daughter Constance is sent against her wishes by her father into the pagan world, with the pope's approval and the sultan's agreement to bring about peace and to give the Christians Jerusalem and free passage "to visit the holy places of the Sepulchre, Mount Calvary, Bethlehem, Nazareth, the Valley of Jehoshaphat, and all other holy places"; she is "ordered" to leave Rome "with great grief, tears, outcry, noise and lament from the whole city."[11] This denial of choice, agency, and voice to the woman is also apparent in the English versions: in Gower, when the sultan, eager to marry Constance, promises to convert to Christianity and sends hostages ("princes sones tuelve," *Confessio Amantis*, ed. Peck, 2.633) as guarantee of his faith, her father, with the blessing of the pope, sends her, despite her

---

[10] "The King of Tars" is the title given in the Auchinleck; in the Vernon and Simeon manuscripts, the poem is titled "The King of Tars and the Soudan of Damas," naming both of the male leads, but not the female protagonist around which the narrative is structured.

[11] Trevet, *Les Cronicles*, ed. Correale and Hamel, pp. 298–300. It is worth remembering that *The King of Tars* was written before Trevet's chronicle, and the differences noted here in Trevet, Gower, and Chaucer are later additions to the tale as presented here.

objections, as bride to the sultan, along with two cardinals, to make sure that the sultan is properly converted. In Chaucer, her objection is even stronger, as Custance weeps and is overcome with sorrow that she, "wrecche womman," must agree to the marriage. As Chaucer's Man of Law puts the matter: "no fors though I spille! / Wommen are born to thraldom and penance, / And to been under mannes governance."[12] But in *Tars*, the emperor's daughter is given full voice, a requirement of the protagonist of both romances and saint's lives. The daughter of Tars takes control of a situation that is rapidly destroying their people and way of life. She acts not for herself but for her whole community and the sake of humanity. But she does act, and her decision, at first appearance "selfless," is in fact both self-fulfilling and culturally salvific in a peculiarly gendered way. Heroines who go outside their home, religion, and culture, perhaps even under "thraldom" (marriage, slavery, etc.), as the Man of Law puts it, have to maintain their integrity — a lonely task in an alien world. This loneliness lies at the heart of the Constance stories, saints' lives like those of Katherine, Margaret, etc. (daughters endangered by headstrong fathers), or Psyche in her wanderings under the persecution of the gods and goddesses in Apuleius's tale, or the stories about Persephone and Alceste in their sojourns in Hades. The true identities of such women often remain hidden through much of the tale, until the appropriate moment when their full power and the society's need for it may be revealed. In *The King of Tars*, the revelation of the princess's Christian identity and the power she has over the sultan lead to the conversion of not only her family, but also her newly-adopted land.

Since religion is of such importance to the poem, hagiography is one model for the narrative. Unlike romances, saints' lives are not distinguished by gender; hagiography is equally comfortable with presenting female and male saints. Many female saints are featured in positions of temporal and spiritual power, and mass conversion is often the result of hagiographic narratives featuring royalty.[13] In *Tars*, the princess's faith is tested, but never found wanting; indeed, her dream vision reassures her, and that reassurance is made flesh in the lump-child. Transformation miracles are at the core of the narrative, separated by a brief didactic description of the basic tenets of Christianity. Though many saints' lives end in martyrdom, happy endings are not necessarily at odds with a religious narrative. In *Tars*, this entails the princess converting the entire sultanate of Damas to Christianity, initially through a demonstration of the power of her religion, then through force of law, and, ultimately, by strength of arms.

However important hagiography is as a source for certain tropes or the audience's generic expectations of the poem, *The King of Tars* is no more a saint's life than it is a romance. The princess is not a saint, though many critics have treated her as one.[14] She

---

[12] Chaucer, Man of Law's Tale, *The Canterbury Tales* II [B¹]285–87, ed. Benson. It is worth noting that in both Gower and Chaucer, the sultan agrees to convert to Christianity as a prerequisite of the marriage, while in *The King of Tars*, the sultan demands the princess convert to Islam before they are wed, though he becomes a Christian in the end.

[13] Of particular resonance here is St. Catherine of Alexandria, a very popular saint, who was the daughter of a king; her legend appears in the Auchinleck manuscript, shortly after *Tars*.

[14] Winstead claims, "*The King of Tars* applauds a 'saint' who stops at nothing to protect her family, obey her husband, and safeguard her people. The only time she opposes her parents is when, for their own good, she insists on marrying the sultan" ("Saints, Wives, and Other 'Hooly Thynges,'" p. 145). Cordery suggests, "The actions of the princess bring about miraculous physical changes . . . Thus the princess is the catalyst not only in saving Christendom but also in spreading the faith

agrees to marry a non-Christian, which no saint would be likely to do. Indeed, to pursue her happy ending, she has to convert falsely and participate in heathen rituals, even though she has not renounced Christ in her heart. The marriage is arranged in order to relieve the political and social suffering of warfare, a war caused by rumor of the princess's beauty and the sultan's lust. There are few Christian values evident here, and yet the sultan has a great victory, rather than a defeat, as befits a pagan villain.

The narrative itself, unlike most saints' lives, features numerous anonymous characters. The poem identifies eight central figures, whose names are necessary for understanding the poem's events.[15] Five of the names come at the end, when the king of Tars and the newly converted sultan of Damas fight five heathen kings; were these five unnamed, it would be difficult to track their actions in the battle.[16] The remaining three characters are named as a necessary feature of baptism, when the baptized are named as part of the ceremony: the child is named for Saint John, on whose day he is brought into Christianity and given human form, and the sultan is named for the priest, Cleophas, who officiates both rites.[17] Unlike saints' lives, where the naming of pious women is crucial, all of the Christian characters in *The King of Tars* are anonymous; this technique increases the resonance with listeners, who can rely on their own imaginations and experiences, rather than thinking of icons or reliquaries. It also distances the narrative from hagiography, which is specifically interested in relating a saint's biography and celebrating that saint's name and devotion. The anonymity of the princess, who is not otherwise named in the text, prevents her from becoming an object of devotion or subject of prayers for intercession. It also removes the tale from the realm of history, and allows a more comfortable discussion of religious doctrine, since it can take place at any time, and is not tied to a specific person, period, or religious movement.

Finally, in attempting to establish the genre of *The King of Tars*, it is worth keeping in mind the fundamentally variable nature of medieval literature. Middle English poems, especially, were usually composed with the end, not the means, in mind.[18] *The King of Tars*

("Medieval Interpretation of Risk," p. 183). As Gilbert argues, both the Vernon and Auchinleck manuscripts suggest "that the Princess would have been morally and generically wrong to have demanded the path of virgin martyrdom at her people's expense, while the greater Christian community within the text is shown ultimately to profit from her marriage just as in hagiography it does from a virgin martyr's death or from a married saint's refusal of worldliness" ("Putting the Pulp into Fiction," p. 116).

[15] The poem also names three saints: Helen (line 155), John (line 730), and Martin (line 802). See the explanatory notes to those lines for more information on their significance.

[16] Indeed, the Vernon scribe had some trouble keeping the lines of action clear, despite the names. In that manuscript, the sultan kills King Carmele twice, and the fate of King Clamadas is omitted because of scribal error. See the appendix for more variants between the Auchinleck and Vernon manuscripts.

[17] The child is named in line 767, the priest in line 919, and the sultan in lines 920–21. See the explanatory notes for more information on the biblical referents for their names.

[18] It is worth considering the fact that Chaucer and Gower are important exceptions because of their investment in the presentation of their tales in *The Canterbury Tales* and *Confessio Amantis*. Both authors carefully prepared their tales within a frame narrative to offer specific context to guide reading. Although the compilers of the manuscripts similarly offer some context for the stories they include,

is best approached as entertainment, with religious doctrine as an important component of understanding. The poem is far from unique in its combination of romance, religion, and didacticism. After an examination of potential sources for tail-rhyme verse, Purdie concludes that the tail-rhyme draws most directly on pious materials and suggests that the form adds spiritual connotations, especially in early romances such as *The King of Tars*.[19] This combination of a religious form with secular materials, of the form of romance with didactic intent, would likely appeal to an audience that was not yet comfortable with straightforward romance or which had specific uses for the poem.

The placement of the poem in the witnesses further illustrates its mixed reception. Medieval readers must have been influenced by the location of texts within a collection, just as modern readers approach texts based on their context.[20] The earliest of the three witnesses, Edinburgh, National Library of Scotland, Advocates' 19.2.1 (the Auchinleck manuscript), places the poem early in the manuscript, following "The Legend of Pope Gregory, the Holy Sinner" and preceding "The Life of Adam and Eve" and lives of Saint Margaret and Saint Katherine.[21] The first item that is not specifically religious is the "Speculum Gy de Warewyke," beginning on folio 39r. Although the Auchinleck manuscript contains many romances and is well known in part because of the large number and high quality of those works, *Tars* is explicitly surrounded by religious texts, unlike the other romances, which appear later and are accompanied by non-religious content, primarily other romances.

The other two witnesses, Oxford, Bodleian Library, Eng.poet.a.1 (the Vernon manuscript) and London, British Library, Additional 22283 (the Simeon manuscript), are much later productions. The Vernon manuscript's interest in religious and didactic texts is clear, leading N. F. Blake to say "the intended audience was a house of nuns or of women who had banded together to establish a small community of a semi-religious nature."[22] Surrounding *The King of Tars* itself are "The Golden Trental," "The Sayings of St. Bernard," and "The Proverbs of the Prophets"; also included in the manuscript are the expanded *Northern Homily Cycle*, *The Prick of Conscience*, the first version of Walter Hilton's *Scale of Perfection*, and the *Ancrene Riwle*.[23] Despite its length and large collection of texts, the Vernon manuscript

---

that context is a scribal decision, not an authorial one, and does not specifically affect the composition of the tales, which existed independently of the manuscript compilation.

[19] See Purdie, *Anglicising Romance*, chapter 2 (pp. 32–65).

[20] Indeed, this seems to be one of the organizing principles of Chaucer's *Canterbury Tales*; as each pilgrim finishes a story, the next pilgrim responds to the tale, creating groups and highlighting certain themes, such as the marriage group. While some manuscripts were the products of opportunity, where texts were copied as they became available, others were clearly carefully organized.

[21] The foliation of the items is "The Legend of Pope Gregory," fols. 1r–6v; *The King of Tars*, fols. 7ra–13vb; "The Life of Adam and Eve," E fols. 1ra–2vb and 14ra–16rb (the first folios were removed from the Auchinleck manuscript and reside in another library); "Seynt Mergrete," fols. 16rb–21ra; and "Seynt Katerine," fols. 21ra–24vb.

[22] Blake, "Vernon MS: Contents and Organisation," p. 58.

[23] The foliation of these items is the expanded *Northern Homily Cycle*, fols. 167r–227v; *The Prick of Conscience*, fols. 265rc–284ra; "The Golden Trental," fols. 303vc–304rc; "The Sayings of St. Bernard," fols. 304rc–304vb; *The King of Tars*, fols. 304vb–307rb; "The Proverbs of the Prophets," fols. 307rb–309va; Hilton's *Scale of Perfection*, fols. 343ra–353va; and *Ancrene Riwle*, fols. 371vb–392rb.

has very few romances, and those tend to be of a religious or didactic nature.[24] The texts in the Simeon manuscript were copied from the Vernon, though they are rearranged for a new, if similar, readership. The Simeon manuscript's "The Kyng of Tars and the Soudan of Damas" follows "The Stacions of Rome," an account of the churches at Rome, where pardons and indulgences were granted to pilgrims, "A Lamentacion that Ure Lady Made to the Cros of hir Soone," and "A Pistel of Susan"; it precedes a collection of twenty-nine hymns and religious songs.[25]

As this brief description of the immediate contents of the manuscripts shows, medieval scribes embedded *The King of Tars* in collections of primarily religious content. Although that context is lost in a single-text edition, it is worth keeping these original frameworks in mind as we read, to heighten our sensitivity to religious motives and motifs in the text. Indeed, using religion as a guide will help clarify some of the more shocking events and illustrate the importance of ritual, especially of baptism.

One key topic that bridges romance and saints' lives is the idea of conversion. *The King of Tars* is definitely a conversion narrative. In some of the Constance stories, the sultan is the one converted, but *Tars* is distinctly different from these tales. In Gower's and Chaucer's Constance stories, no mention is made of what happens to the soul of the converted sultan after his mother murders him.[26] It is worth noting, however, that in both tales, the sultan converts at the promptings of lust; that is, he adopts Christianity solely to wed the Christian princess without guilt. There is a stark difference between the sultan here and Alla, in Chaucer's Man of Law's Tale, who converts because he sincerely believes in the truth of Christianity. After Alla is converted in Northumbria, the fate of his adoption of Christianity becomes a powerful component of the narrative, as he undergoes penance and travels to Rome for absolution, by which means he is ultimately reconciled with his God and family. That recovery experience ends in an affirmation of faith. Unlike these later tales, *The King of Tars* expressly focuses on the conversion of the sultan, offering a false conversion in the person of the princess, and bringing all the principal figures to Christianity in the end.

BAPTISM

The King of Tars features two baptisms, and the role they play is more than simply inducting two more souls into the faith; they physically reform the baptized in stunning shows of the empowerment of Christianity. The first baptism concerns the miraculous lump-child (lines 760–68). Upon its christening, the lump-child

> . . . hadde liif and lim and fas   *life; limb; face*
> And crid with gret deray,   *cried; great commotion*

---

[24] The romances included in the Vernon manuscript are *The King of Tars* (fols. 304vb–307rb), "Robert of Sicily" (fols. 300rc–301rc), "Ypotis" (fols. 296va–297vc), and "Joseph of Arimathea" (fols. 403ra–404vb).

[25] The foliation of these items is "The Stacions of Rome," fol. 123r–124v; "A Lamentacion that Ure Lady," fol. 124v–125v; "A Pistel of Susan," fols. 125v–126r; *The King of Tars*, fols. 126rc–128va; and hymns, fols. 128v–134v.

[26] Both Gower (*Confessio Amantis* 2.688–92, ed. Peck) and Chaucer (The Man of Law's Tale, *The Canterbury Tales* II[B¹] 428–30, ed. Benson) immediately turn their attention to Constance's exile after the feasting people are slain.

And hadde hide and flesche and fel   *skin*
And alle that ever therto bifel   *to this happened*
    (lines 770–73)

The baptismal waters induct the lump of flesh into the faith, and in so doing, the lump gains a father, the Father, to replace the sultan's failed paternity. The child is quickly inspired, and he cries loudly, a sign of his new life. Moreover, as befits a true child of God, the baby is a beautiful boy: "Feirer child might non be bore — / It no hadde never [*had never*] a lime forlore [*lost*] / Wele schapen it was" (lines 775–77). This miracle demonstrates the vitality of Christianity: the sultan's gods could not endow the child with form, but Christianity has endowed it with perfect form. This leads to the second, equally astonishing baptism, that of the sultan.

When he sees the lump-child's new beauty, the sultan, true to his word, agrees to accept Christianity. It is through the miracle of the child's fleshy conversion that the sultan acknowledges the power of Christ, and this religious conversion could be read as a reverse-birth, that is, the sultan is spiritually the son of his own child. To prepare for his formal conversion, the sultan hears a brief description of the tenets of Christianity (lines 836–67), receives some further instruction from a priest, and is baptized himself, leading to another significant metamorphosis:

His hide that blac and lothely was   *loathly*
Al white bicom thurth Godes gras   *through; grace*
    And clere withouten blame.
And when the soudan seye that sight,   *saw*
Than leved he wele on God almight;   *believed*
    His care went to game.   *turned into mirth*
    (lines 922–27)

This baptism cleanses the sultan of sin, and, in so doing, it removes his "blac and lothely" hide. He now sees himself as white, cleaned of sin and the shame it implies. This is not a simple statement of race as we understand it today; instead, it is a fairly well-developed conception of the overriding blessing of Christianity, and it also reflects a specific understanding of baptism that was current in the fourteenth century.

Walter Hilton describes the power of baptism as one that restores shape. In *The Scale of Perfection*, he says that sins "maken a soule to lese [*lose*] the schap and the liknesse of God."[27] For Hilton, a conservative Augustinian, contemplation was a means to "assist in the recovery in the individual of the image of God that has been distorted by sin."[28] Baptism was the first step in restoring the divine image, and that image is on full display in this text. The child, who was truly fatherless, is given form; as Hilton notes,

the soule of a childe that is born and is uncristened, bicause of the origynal synne hath no liknesse of God; he is not but an image of the feend and a brond [*firebrand*] of helle. But as soone as it is cristened, it is reformed to the ymage of God, and thorugh vertu of feith of

---

[27] Hilton, *Scale of Perfection*, ed. Bestul, Book II, chapter 6, line 230 (p. 143); the gloss is mine.

[28] Bestul, introduction to Hilton, *Scale of Perfection*, p. 3.

Holi Chirche sodeynli is turned fro the liknes of the feend and maad like to an angel of hevene.[29]

Hilton's description of monstrosity is spiritual, not physical, although *The King of Tars* literalizes this philosophical point. The lump-child is not specifically demonic in its appearance, but the lack of defining characteristics is foul enough to disturb all who look upon it. It is certainly not physically or spiritually formed in the image of God until its baptism, at which point it becomes a beautiful boy.

The sultan is similarly disturbing in appearance. His skin is not just black, it is a loathly hide, physically likening him to an animal. He is sinful and has willfully dwelt apart from God. Through baptism, he is cleansed of his sins and made a shining example of the power of Christian belief, and thus, for a medieval English audience, well-formed and white, like themselves. Again, Hilton sums up the philosophy behind the sultan's sudden transformation:

> Also the same falleth [*happens*] to a Jewe or in a Sarceyn, whiche or [*before*] thei be cristened aren not but manciples [*stewards*] of helle, but whanne thei forsaken ther [*their*] errour and fallen mekeli to the trouthe in Crist, and receyven the baptym of water in the Holi Goost, soothli withouten ony taryyinge thei aren reformed to the liknesse of God."[30]

The sultan explicitly accepts Christianity "with gode wille" (line 916), and it is the good intention of that willingness that orthodox thinkers like Hilton celebrated. The sultan is under no coercion, but he recognizes the power of Christianity as displayed through his child's transformation, and his new belief is reinforced by his own physical and spiritual transformation. The orthodox belief in the authority of the spirit to transform the flesh is made literal, and that literalization is a crucial feature of the narrative.

Ultimately, the key to understanding these transformations rather than being repulsed by the simplicity of their racial overtone is to remember that baptism "affects not only the soul," as Anna Czarnowus argues, "but also the bodies of newly baptized Christians, while here it didactically produces an infant as beautiful as its non-heathen mother."[31] Indeed, the lump-child's religion is written on its body, and this inscription later affects the sultan in a similarly breathtaking transformation. The monstrous child indicates "its father's sinfulness" and leads, through the body, "to reconciliation between Islam and Christianity. . . . The formless body symbolizes the uselessness of Muslim beliefs, or perhaps even their harmfulness for the health of one's body and spirit."[32] The importance of race is not in its biological immutability, but in its presentation of the inner belief writ on the body itself. In *The King of Tars*, baptism is able to wash away the stain of sin from anyone. The monstrous lump-child serves as a warning to the sultan of Damas that all is not right in his household, and its transformation "constitutes . . . an encouragement to subject oneself to baptism."[33]

---

[29] Hilton, *Scale of Perfection*, ed. Bestul, Book II, chapter 6, lines 236–41 (p. 143); gloss is original.

[30] Hilton, *Scale of Perfection*, ed. Bestul, Book II, chapter 6, lines 241–44 (pp. 143–44); glosses are original.

[31] Czarnowus, "'Stille as Ston,'" p. 472.

[32] Czarnowus, "'Stille as Ston,'" p. 473.

[33] Czarnowus, "'Stille as Ston,'" p. 473.

As a result of the child's baptism, miraculous transformations occur that lead to the wholesale conversion of a people and the expansion of Christian power in the Middle East.

RACE AND TRANSFORMATION

Perhaps the most striking events of the poem occur as a result of baptism: the transformation of lump-child to beautiful boy and the purification of the sultan written on his skin. Although both events directly portray the authority of Christianity, the transformations are predicated on ideas more complicated than they appear on the surface. Both the child and the sultan are monsters indicative of improper belief, but neither should be read as simply a statement of Caucasian or Christian superiority. It is important to recognize the religious lens of these transformations in order to understand the spiritual tensions present in the work.

In an article on race in the Middle Ages, Thomas Hahn notes that for a medieval audience, race was not the ultimate trope of difference between people.[34] *The King of Tars* certainly goes beyond race; Christianity is able to overcome all physical difference, giving form to the shapeless lump-child and transforming the sultan from "blac and lothely" to "Al white . . . and clere."[35] Clearly, race here is not an immutable characteristic, but an external signifier of internal being and belief. When the princess pretends to convert to Islam in lines 463–501, she undergoes no physical change, remaining the beauty that caused the poem's initial conflict. Indeed, the next stanza (lines 502–13) notes that, though she knew the heathen law and performed its rites, she never abandoned Christianity,[36] and the poem never describes any physical change because neither her faith nor her spirit have changed. However, when the sultan is baptized, his skin miraculously changes color and condition, marking his new perception of himself. Following this, his people never remark upon his transformation; they seem to be unaware of his conversion, despite this physical alteration that marks his spiritual change. Even when the conversion is made clear, and the sultan demands his people convert or die, there is no indication that the people of Damas recognize the sultan's transformation:

Mani Sarrazin stout and bold	*Saracens*
That in his court were,	
Mani seyd that thai wold,	
And mani seyd that thai nold	*would not*
Be cristned in non maner.	*no way*
(lines 1040–44)	

The poem does not mention the sultan's physical change here; it only says that many Saracens converted, because they implicitly recognize the power of Christianity through the sultan's transformation and because they value their vows of fealty and respect the sultan's

---

[34] Hahn, "Difference the Middle Ages Makes," p. 6.

[35] The child's transformation from lump to well-formed child occurs in lines 769–77; the sultan's transformation, quoted here, occurs in lines 922–24.

[36] In this regard, she is similar to the Old Testament figure Judith, who agrees to conjoin with Holofernes, but until he wins the victory over the Jews in Bethulia, she will continue to practice her Jewish rites.

commandment. Conversely, many said they would not convert, and they were summarily executed. But the poem offers no further remarks on the sultan's appearance, instead shifting its focus from the religiously driven miracle of transformation to a romance-style war of conversion.

Two philosophical threads come together to help explain the silence of both characters and story. First, as Hahn notes, color was not the default for "race" in the Middle Ages; indeed, one aspect of the Constance tale, of which *The King of Tars* is a fairly early version, is the understanding that a black man can fall in love with a white woman based solely on physical descriptions. This being the case, color might not have a strong influence on interactions with different people, and therefore it would not be considered as important a factor as modern readers might expect. The other factor worth considering is the medieval scientific theory of skin color. Hahn summarizes the theory of skin color as it was applied to Ethiopians in medieval encyclopedias by noting that Isidore of Seville and Bartholomew the Englishman both ascribe dark skin to the influence of climate.[37] This leads to a theory that skin color is mutable, a theory that is not entirely without scientific precedent: skin can darken or lighten, becoming tan or pale in response to the effect of exposure to sunlight. The current poem goes much further along this trajectory, however, ascribing the change not to melanin production but instead to religion, complementing scientific observation with religious application. Nor is *The King of Tars* unique in this racial shift.

Just before he briefly discusses the conversion of the sultan in *The King of Tars*, Hahn notes that skin color changes in *Cursor Mundi*, where King David "converts monstrous blacks to flawless whites."[38] This change is possible in part because of a spiritual understanding of the difference in skin color. While discussing the monstrous difference of Ethiopians, Paulinus of Nola "explained that the Ethiopians had been scorched by sin and vice rather than by the sun," as in the myth of Phaeton.[39] Such a belief would easily lead to a conflation of the theoretical and the physical, explaining the sultan's change from black to white as a cleansing of sin in the baptismal waters. Tales brought back from the Crusades could also have contributed to the strength or spread of this theory. The English audience for whom the poem was written would have believed their faith to be the only completely true one. Tales of Greek Orthodox rites and belief would have seemed to be sinful, in that the religion was mistaken about some details, but true to the essential character of Christianity. Accordingly, Mediterranean skin tones are generally darker than British ones. Another step away is the Holy Land, populated with people of a decidedly different religion, and darker skin tones yet. Finally, the people of Africa have the darkest skin tones, and the least connection to or interest in Christianity. And they are also the most deformed people in the world, according to the encyclopedists and cartographers of the Middle Ages, who place them in the marginal areas of the world.[40]

---

[37] Hahn, "Difference the Middle Ages Makes," p. 11.

[38] Hahn, "Difference the Middle Ages Makes," p. 14. The edition Hahn cites is *Cursor Mundi*, ed. Morris, lines 8071–8122 (pp. 466–68).

[39] Quoted by Cohen, "Monster Culture (Seven Theses)," p. 10.

[40] The marginal placement of the strange races has been noted by numerous scholars, often referring back to Friedman's *Monstrous Races in Medieval Art and Thought*, especially chapter 3. Many medieval world maps offer visual analogs, placing most of the strangest races on the edge of the African continent, far from Jerusalem, the spiritual center of the world.

However, just as the English, who are also placed on the edge of Europe, are beautiful and, most importantly, Christian, so too can these distant, strange people become beautiful through abandoning their false, sinful beliefs and converting to Christianity. The conventional beauty of the princess of Tars, an enclave of Christianity in the East, attests to this possibility, and it is demonstrated in the baptisms of both sultan and child. Indeed, as Czarnowus notes, the sultan's undesirability is not strictly or even primarily physical — the problem is that his actions and his beliefs are repugnant, almost bestial.[41] The sultan's outbursts are very physical, and he is at first described as wild as a boar (line 98); further, he, along with all other Saracens, is repeatedly likened to a hound. With his baptism, not only is his corporeal form changed, but also his personality; rather than being a rough, violent heathen, the sultan becomes much more calm and deliberate in his actions, relying on reason and patience instead of sudden, violent action to convert his people. Nonetheless, although the newly baptized sultan relies initially on reason and patience, he shows no mercy to those who will not convert, and he beheads them swiftly. This is not the passionate action of a raging mind, but the controlled action of a calculating ruler. This psychological change parallels the physical change that resulted from his conversion, further distancing the transformation from the surface reading of racism.

Although race is not an insurmountable sign of difference, the sultan and princess are of radically different religious backgrounds, and miscegenation is the result. Czarnowus argues that the monstrosity of the lump-child "exposes the dire consequences of violating the taboo against marriages between whites and non-whites," and thus "miscegenation" is the best term for the coupling, despite its anachronism.[42] However, the sultan's skin color is not described until the child has been baptized, at which time his blackness is mentioned, and that perhaps for rhyme: "Than cam the soudan that was blac, / And sche schewed him the child and spac" (lines 793–94). After a brief discussion of Christian doctrine, the sultan is baptized, and his skin color emphasizes the miracle and truth of his conversion:

> His hide that blac and lothely was   *loathly*
> Al white bicom thurth Godes gras   *through; grace*
>   And clere withouten blame.
> And when the soudan seye that sight,   *saw*
> Than leved he wele on God almight;   *believed*
>   His care went to game.   *turned into mirth*
>   (lines 922–27)

The sultan's blackness is simply not an issue until the narrative has come to the conversion miracle. Were this poem interested in highlighting racial difference, the sultan's skin color would have been described long before the lump-child's beauty had been realized through the agency of religion. Instead, the sultan's skin is only important as an outward sign of his inner being, and, for the poet and his intended audience, that being has been purified and beautified by Christianity. However, the sultan's purification is the second miracle in the text, and it pales in comparison to the child's transformation, which establishes the correctness of Christianity and initiates the sultan's conversion.

---

[41] Czarnowus, "'Stille as Ston,'" pp. 469–70.

[42] Czarnowus, "'Stille as Ston,'" p. 465.

THE CHILD

An "outrageously sensational"[43] character in the tale, the child who is born "a rond of flesche yschore" (line 577) exceeds the monstrosity of its analogues.[44] Jane Gilbert observes that "the analogues present the lump primarily as its father's child," but *The King of Tars*, especially as presented in the Auchinleck manuscript, "draws on Aristotelian conception theory" to deprive the child of his father's role.[45] Aristotelian theory describes conception as one "in which the mother contributes only the basic matter, the material, fleshy substance" and "the father, through his seed, supplies the 'life or spirit or form,' the vital principle which transforms the matter into a human child and animates it."[46] When the parents are somehow incompatible, the child born is monstrous; quite often, it is physically mixed, such as Fierfiz in Wolfram von Eschenbach's *Parzival*, who is black with white spots.[47] Drawing on both Aristotle and Lacan, Gilbert describes the science behind the lump-child's form in an effort to explain the child's transformation through the establishment of a religious paternity. The lump-child further complicates the racial charge of the poem, and like the transformation of the sultan, the child's ugliness, that is, its formlessness, reflects its parents' religious, not biological, difference.

In this poem, the child has substance or matter, supplied by the mother, but no form or life, which is supplied by the father. The application of Aristotelian conception theory is clear: the child is born a lump of flesh, without any organizing principle and without life; that is, the father's role in this pregnancy has been deformed. However, as Gilbert points out, even if the lump has "no paternal input at all," the sultan's parenthood is never in question.[48] Despite this certainty, the sultan insistently chides his wife — the formless child is not his fault, but hers, as his is the dominant culture. Further, she is deceptive, he argues, because she keeps her true faith from her husband and merely performs Saracen rites without imbuing them with any true sentiment. Thus, the princess is the party at fault.

---

[43] Gilbert, "Putting the Pulp into Fiction," p. 102.

[44] The analogues are described in Hornstein's work, especially her dissertation, "Study of Historical and Folk-lore Sources," and her "New Analogues" article. Hornstein's findings were summarized by Shores, *The King of Tars: A New Edition*, pp. 38–42. Briefly, Hornstein sorts monstrous births into three categories: hairy births; half-and-half births (itself subdivided into three types: half-hairy; half-human, half-animal; and half-black, half-white ["New Analogues," p. 434]), and formless lumps. Only *The King of Tars* and Giovanni Villani's *Istorie Fiorentine*, an Italian chronicle, present the child as a formless lump.

[45] Gilbert, "Putting the Pulp into Fiction," p. 105.

[46] Gilbert wrote an article considering paternity in both *The King of Tars* and *Sir Gowther* ("Unnatural Mothers and Monstrous Children"), and later focused her comments on *The King of Tars* in another article ("Putting the Pulp into Fiction") which forms the basis for the following discussion. This description of the child is from Gilbert, "Putting the Pulp into Fiction," p. 102.

[47] In this German text, Fierfiz is the half-brother of Parzival. They share the same Christian father, but Feirefiz's mother is Belacane, a heathen queen. When he was born, Wolfram describes him as "of two colors and in whom God had wrought a marvel, for he was both black and white. Immediately the queen kissed him over and over again on his white spots. . . . Like a magpie was the color of his hair and of his skin" (*Parzival*, pp. 32–33).

[48] Gilbert, "Putting the Pulp into Fiction," p. 106.

But his denial of fault in the paternity is complicated by two factors: religion and character. Critics often compare the lump-child to a bear, whose offspring, according to bestiaries, were born as lumps of flesh that the mother bear would lick into shape.[49] Although the lump's mother, the princess, does give the lump a proper form, her means is Christianity, not licking. And though the sultan is never described as a bear, he is explicitly likened to a boar (line 98), and all Saracens are likened to hounds. Thus, the sultan's animal characteristics may lead to an animal-like child. Despite these resonances with animals as they were understood through bestiaries, the overriding concern of the poem is religious, and that is more important for the interpretation of the poem because the formlessness is not grounded in physical mixing but in spiritual incompatibility.

Czarnowus implicitly identifies this role for religion, though she presents it in terms of race, observing that for the sultan, "the lump-like infant exposes its mother's false conversion rather than his own ethnic difference."[50] As discussed above, race is less important as a sign of difference than is religion, since race can be changed with conversion. Returning to the matter of fault, Czarnowus points out that the princess "cannot, however, be the cause of her offspring's possible monstrosity due to her impeccability."[51] Indeed, for a Christian audience, the princess is hard to fault. Her actions are not only reasonable for self-preservation, they have divine approval through the dream. Despite the sultan's correct accusation of falsity, the princess is never presented in a negative light: she decides to end the war, she reasons with her parents to allow her to marry the sultan, she has a dream in which Christ Himself speaks to her; indeed, her only fault is her subterfuge in pretending to convert to Islam, but even that sin is minimized in the narrative, as it has divine approval and a positive conclusion. And the child born to the true, almost saintly princess is purely hers; the faulty party in the birth is the father, who is unable to offer spiritual shape, rather than the mother, who properly produces the fleshy matter. That is, "it is the father's religious and racial alterity" that results "in disturbing the natural growth of the child in its the princess's [sic] womb."[52] The power of Christianity is paramount, and the princess is faithful, so the fault must lie with the heathen sultan.

The sultan's inability to imbue his child with form ultimately leads to his own conversion. As Czarnowus notes, "the shapeless child thus demonstrates deficiency on the part of the sultan."[53] His inability initially seems to be biological; that is, he cannot naturally give form to his child because of a fundamental incompatibility with the princess. But more importantly, his inability is religious: although he prays to his gods, in whom he has no lack of faith, they are unable to imbue the lump-child with form; that is, the Saracen gods are unable to step in and become fathers to this child of miscegenation. That role is reserved for the Father, that is, the Christian God, whose spiritual paternity is established through baptism. The sultan has no right to fatherhood, be it physical or spiritual, because he does not acknowledge Christianity, the most important criterion in the poem. As Gilbert states,

---

[49] For one description of the bear, see *Bestiary*, trans. Barber, p. 59. On the poem's allusion to the bear, see, e.g., "*The King of Tars*: A New Edition," ed. Shores, pp. 82–84 and 208n577a, 538v; Gilbert, "Putting the Pulp into Fiction," p. 104; and Czarnowus, "'Stille as Ston,'" p. 472.

[50] Czarnowus, "'Stille as Ston,'" p. 472.

[51] Czarnowus, "'Stille as Ston,'" p. 469.

[52] Czarnowus, "'Stille as Ston,'" p. 469.

[53] Czarnowus, "'Stille as Ston,'" p. 472.

"the paternity lacking pertains not to the Sultan's acknowledged physical fatherhood but to his right to be named as the child's father."[54] The text gives us no reason to think that the sultan is not part of this child: his paternity, his role as father, is not questioned. Indeed, the plot develops in line with his paternity: the princess is wed, and three months later, she is impregnated; forty weeks after that, she gives birth. Biologically, the sultan is the only candidate to be the child's father. However, according to this text, the physical act of childbirth is not enough to bring the mixed family together; they must all be born into Christianity through baptism, and it is that sacrament that introduces the miracles that lead the poem to its conclusion. The sultan's inability to give his child form, through either biology or religion, leads him to recognize the incompatibility of his family, and he takes steps to unify them through his own conversion to Christianity.

This hybrid family, especially the child, is an excellent metaphor for the poem itself. A formless mass, a union of two distinct parents, is unified by religion, and this union brings form and function. The poem, a hybrid of hagiography and romance, is given clear form and purpose when read through a religious lens, making its ugliness, if not beautiful, then at least meaningful and pointed.

MANUSCRIPT WITNESSES

Three manuscripts contain copies of *The King of Tars*: Edinburgh, National Library of Scotland, Advocates' 19.2.1 (fols. 7ra–13vb), better known as the Auchinleck manuscript; Oxford, Bodleian Library, Eng.poet.a.1 (fols. 304vb–307ra), the Vernon manuscript; and London, British Library, Additional 22283 (fols. 126rc–128va), the Simeon manuscript. The Auchinleck manuscript is the oldest of the three witnesses, but based on lacunae in the text and the vast differences between it and the other witnesses, scholarly consensus holds that it does not contain the original version of the poem. The Simeon manuscript has been described as a fairly straightforward copy of the Vernon, with scribal errors but little if any conscious scribal modification of the text.[55]

I have chosen the Auchinleck manuscript as the base-text for this edition. The variants present in the Vernon and Simeon manuscripts, while inherently interesting, are often inferior, and reflect a variety of scribal changes, from simple dialectical differences and scribal errors to large-scale textual revision. Judith Perryman, in her 1980 edition, defends the priority of the Auchinleck "on the basis of the small amount of omission, absence of confused sense, and the uniformity of stanza form."[56] The Auchinleck is also the oldest of the three manuscripts. To help illustrate the more significant changes made to the text copied into Vernon, see the appendix.[57]

---

[54] Gilbert, "Putting the Pulp into Fiction," p. 108.

[55] For a list of the variants between Vernon and Simeon manuscripts, see "*The King of Tars*: A New Edition," ed. Shores, where she presents them in footnotes, along with an appendix correcting Krause's errors in representing Simeon (p. 216).

[56] *The King of Tars*, ed. Perryman, p. 31.

[57] Gilbert also offers a summary discussion of the differences in "Putting the Pulp into Fiction," pp. 112–19.

AUCHINLECK

This manuscript was compiled in the 1330s and is "best known for its early and often unique texts of the metrical romances, though its contents range widely, to include lives of saints, doctrinal exposition, a collection of tales, works of social comment, and a chronicle."[58] Eugen Kölbing brought the manuscript to the attention of critics in 1884, and F. Krause edited a series of texts from the Auchinleck manuscript, including *The King of Tars*, after the publication of Kölbing's article. One of the most influential articles on the manuscript came in 1940, when Laura Hibbard Loomis put forth a theory that Chaucer himself read the manuscript, and that the texts contained therein were directly influential on his Tale of Sir Thopas in *The Canterbury Tales*.[59] Alison Wiggins, fairly skeptical of this argument, summarizes it as "a theory based partly on circumstantial evidence (the Auchinleck was produced in London c.1331–40 and Chaucer was born in the city at about this time, c.1340)" and partly on a "claim for verbal similarities between The Tale of Sir Thopas and the Auchinleck stanzaic Guy of Warwick."[60] Loomis's article inspired a great deal of romantic interest in the manuscript as a physical link with a foundational poet, and increased interest in the manuscript as an object and potential source for Chaucer. Wiggins does, however, allow the specter of Chaucer to bolster the Auchinleck's reputation, writing "Auchinleck is especially valuable for understanding the development of English literature because it offers an insight into an English vernacular literary culture which preceded and was influential upon Chaucer and his generation."[61] Much like *The Canterbury Tales*, the Auchinleck manuscript is an important miscellany of texts. While it is likely impossible to prove any direct influence on Chaucer, the manuscript presents the kind of literary background he expected of his audience, and with which he himself was working.

So even if we abandon Loomis's powerfully attractive myth of direct influence, the Auchinleck manuscript remains vitally important to Middle English literature. Oliver Pickering identifies it as one of "the two major anthologies of Middle English writing compiled in the first half of the fourteenth century,"[62] and Ralph Hanna, a champion of manuscript study, acknowledges the manuscript's unavoidable place in discussions of London literary production before Chaucer.[63] Many theories have circulated regarding its production, most in support or in opposition of Loomis's "bookshop theory."[64] Loomis opened this discussion by arguing the Auchinleck manuscript was produced in a bookshop modeled on a monastic scriptorium, relying on a team of scribes copying the texts to

---

[58] Turville-Petre, *England the Nation*, p. 108.

[59] Loomis, "Chaucer and the Auchinleck MS."

[60] Wiggins, "Auchinleck Manuscript: Importance."

[61] Wiggins, "Auchinleck Manuscript: Importance."

[62] Pickering, "Stanzaic Verse," p. 287. The other manuscript he describes in this phrase is London, British Library, MS Harley 2253.

[63] Hanna, "Reconsidering the Auchinleck Manuscript," p. 92; he calls the manuscript "the one early London English book one cannot escape (although I had long hoped I would)."

[64] Hanna, "Reconsidering the Auchinleck Manuscript," briefly reviews the major positions on pp. 93–94, before putting forth his own speculation that the book was a "special order" created for a client who requested various pieces, which were copied primarily by one scribe (p. 94).

produce the manuscript.[65] This was the generally held position until Timothy A. Shonk's work in the 1980s.[66] He used the manuscript's organizational features to argue that the primary scribe was the editor of the volume, copying much of the text and overseeing its assembly, acting as liaison between the scribes and the purchaser. Most recently, Hanna suggests the manuscript was primarily the work of one scribe who called in friends to help out as needed.[67] Given the early date for the manuscript, all of these are viable theories, but they all avoid the question of patronage and ownership.

Setting aside the debates over the manuscript's creation and early ownership, the texts themselves, as individual pieces and as a collected volume, are worth renewed attention. In *England the Nation*, Thorlac Turville-Petre argues that the Auchinleck is a highly themed manuscript intended to help establish an English identity through patriotic expression, and he describes the Auchinleck as a "carefully organized manuscript" for which "there was an editor who took responsibility not only for selecting and organizing the material, but also for reworking and adapting some texts."[68] Similarly, Siobhain Bly Calkin, in a monograph centered on studying the manuscript's creation of "Englishness," notes the Auchinleck "has long been recognized as one of the most important vernacular English manuscripts" before Chaucer.[69] Wiggins describes the manuscript as "perhaps the first example of a collection specifically designed for enthusiasts of literary and historical texts in the English language."[70] But perhaps the most compelling reason for my choice of base text is that, in addition to the general interest in the manuscript, its version of *The King of Tars* is well-written and lacks many of the difficulties the other witnesses introduce.

VERNON AND SIMEON

In an article on the Vernon and Simeon manuscripts, "the two largest Middle English anthologies of verse and prose," A. I. Doyle compares the contents of the two in general, theoretical categories in an effort to consider the specific relationship between them.[71] Though the article is brief, Doyle raises many issues which have not yet been carefully investigated. Doyle concludes that the Simeon is a defective copy of the Vernon, with changes and omissions resulting from scribal alteration and error and the vicissitudes of time.[72] The majority of editors of *The King of Tars* have long observed this characteristic of

---

[65] Loomis, "Auchinleck Manuscript and a Possible London Bookshop."

[66] Shonk, "Study of the Auchinleck Manuscript: Bookmen and Bookmaking."

[67] Hanna, "Reconsidering the Auchinleck Manuscript," p. 94.

[68] Turville-Petre, *England the Nation*, pp. 109 and 112.

[69] Calkin, *Saracens and the Making of English Identity*, p. 4.

[70] Wiggins, "Auchinleck Manuscript: Importance."

[71] Doyle, "Shaping of the Vernon and Simeon Manuscripts," p. 328. He describes his division of Vernon into five parts, identifying them "by the points at which the items end and begin at quire-changes" (p. 329).

[72] Though many leaves of the Simeon manuscript have been lost, its structure and contents strongly parallel Vernon, though it is not an exact copy. Interested readers should consult the facsimile of Vernon, which discusses the parallels between the two in detail.

Simeon's text, and some have focused on Vernon as their base text when presenting the tradition witnessed by these two manuscripts, using the Simeon solely in the apparatus.

Like the Auchinleck, the Vernon manuscript is a remarkable work. It is, "both in physical size and by the number of its contents, the biggest surviving volume of Middle English writings (with a small amount of Anglo-Norman and Latin), for many of which it has the earliest and for some the sole known copy."[73] Despite its size, Doyle suggests the manuscript is too carefully constructed to be a miscellany of texts copied as they became available, though he allows that the collection of texts is too broad to strongly support a single intended readership.[74] As mentioned above, the text of *The King of Tars* present in the Vernon manuscript follows "The Sayings of St. Bernard" and precedes "The Proverbs of Prophets," placing the work in a clearly religious context, a context that is largely supported by the rest of the manuscript, which opens with the *South English Legendary* and includes an A-text of Langland's *Piers Plowman*, *The Prick of Conscience*, the first book of Walter Hilton's *Scale of Perfection*, and the *Ancrene Riwle*. It is remarkably light on romances, including only *Ypotis*, *Robert of Sicily*, and a partial text of *Joseph of Arimathea* in addition to *The King of Tars*.

Doyle notes that events of 1384 are included in the text, though he is careful not to date the manuscript more precisely than to suggest the late 1380s as the earliest date for completion of the manuscript. Unlike the Auchinleck manuscript, which includes at least six distinct hands, only two scribes worked on the Vernon manuscript: scribe A supplied rubrics and a table of contents after scribe B had completed copying the texts contained in the manuscript.[75] The Simeon manuscript is generally dated to a period shortly after the Vernon; Shores suggests the manuscript "dates from the period between 1380 and 1400."[76] Although the texts of *Tars* are very similar, Perryman notes fifty-five textual variants between the Vernon and Simeon manuscripts, "all of which are trivial," primarily minor orthographic differences.[77]

TEXTUAL RELATIONSHIPS BETWEEN THE WITNESSES

Though the text of *The King of Tars* preserved in the Auchinleck is the oldest of the three written copies, it is not the earliest rendition of the narrative. However, as Laura A. Hibbard notes, it "is probably not much later than the original version."[78] Although the story itself is incomplete, as some lines have been lost at the end of the text, a comparison to the versions in the Vernon and Simeon manuscripts suggests that there is little missing. However, it is possible that the Auchinleck manuscript originally had a more complex ending than that in the Vernon and the Simeon, which abruptly finish the tale in two stanzas after the last of the

---

[73] Doyle, "Introduction," p. 1.

[74] Doyle, "Introduction," pp. 14–15.

[75] Doyle, "Introduction," p. 5. He suggests the main scribe of the Vernon manuscript, scribe B, is the same hand who is identified as scribe 2 of the Simeon manuscript ("Shaping of the Vernon and Simeon Manuscripts," p. 329), which may help explain the similarities of the two manuscripts, and further relegates the Simeon to a position of secondary importance as a witness.

[76] "*The King of Tars*: A New Edition," ed. Shores, p. 19.

[77] *The King of Tars*, ed. Perryman, p. 27.

[78] Hibbard, *Mediæval Romance in England*, p. 45.

heathen kings is killed.[79] Unfortunately, there is no way to know for certain how much has been lost from the end of the Auchinleck manuscript's *Tars*, though it is probably not much.

Past editors of this text have chosen to use both the Auchinleck and Vernon manuscripts as base texts for various reasons. Shores argues for the importance of the Vernon on the grounds that it offers a more difficult, and therefore more literary, reading;[80] conversely, Perryman argues against using the Vernon or the Simeon as a base text. After discussing some of the most egregious textual problems, she concludes that the Auchinleck manuscript "has no such glaring errors of sense, and it omits only eight lines of text" present in the Vernon and the Simeon.[81] Further, the Auchinleck has a more consistent rhyme scheme, deviating from the pattern only once, whereas in the Vernon and Simeon manuscripts, "sixteen of the ninety-four stanzas" have different rhyme patterns.[82] Although the two versions agree on all the major plot elements and the basic structure of the narrative, they "differ too much to permit a reconstruction of the textual tradition"; of the 1122 lines of the text in the Vernon and Simeon manuscripts, only 191 are identical and parallel to the Auchinleck's; of the remaining 890 similar lines, the variations are often minor. The Vernon and Simeon versions omit a number of lines, including nine complete stanzas and parts of five others; these changes introduce some logical problems, as the plot is no longer complete.[83] Given the earlier witness, the superior prosody, and the more consistent narrative, the Auchinleck text is the best text for a modern edition.

PREVIOUS EDITIONS

The King of Tars has been edited seven times before the current work. The two earliest editors, Thomas Warton and Joseph Ritson, read the poem through an antiquarian's lens. Warton's edition is based on the Vernon manuscript, and offers extracts woven together with a somewhat convoluted summary. Ritson offers a full edition of the Vernon, though he adds some lines from the Auchinleck to fill in narrative gaps. Neither edition is particularly scholarly by modern standards; though both editors produced competent transcriptions, they took some liberties with spelling, and despite including some notes, neither offers

---

[79] It is also possible that both the Auchinleck and Vernon manuscripts were copied from an exemplar that itself lacked an ending, leading the Vernon scribe to quickly generate a conclusion to the narrative, the way some scribes did for Chaucer's Cook's Tale.

[80] "*The King of Tars*: A New Edition," ed. Shores, pp. 88–135, esp. pp. 94–97.

[81] *The King of Tars*, ed. Perryman, p. 30. The two textual problems she discusses occur in lines 1160–76, where, during the final battle scene, the Vernon and Simeon manuscripts omit lines 1160–66, "which means that here the king of Tars goes to the defence of the sultan without cause, and he strikes down for a second time the sultan's already vanquished opponent." She also refers to lines 655–58, where the sultan beats his gods, observing that "Jove appears twice in one list, and Tirmagaunt is apparently his own brother" in Vernon and Simeon (p. 30).

[82] *The King of Tars*, ed. Perryman, p. 31. The standard rhyme pattern for the text is *aabaabccbddb*; the Auchinleck's lines 694–705 rhyme *aabaabccbccb*. According to Perryman, there are five variants from this scheme present in the Vernon and Simeon manuscripts.

[83] *The King of Tars*, ed. Perryman, p. 29. See the appendix for a presentation of the lines missing from the Auchinleck manuscript.

anything "approaching a full critical apparatus."[84] Ritson's text was the only complete printed edition until the end of the nineteenth century, when F. Krause published an edition of the Auchinleck and Vernon texts in parallel as part of his series publishing works from the Auchinleck manuscript.[85] Doris Shores politely but firmly lists the problems with Krause's edition; in brief, Krause's readings are occasionally wrong, and his editorial method is inconsistent throughout.[86] Despite these deficiencies, Krause's edition remained the standard for nearly a century.

During that time, three students produced dissertations editing the text. The first, by Robert J. Geist, is modeled on Krause's work, offering an edition of both the Auchinleck and Vernon texts; "his reading follows Krause's almost to the letter," as Shores notes, and she reports his opinion that the dissertation and two articles on the poem "constitute his contribution to the subject."[87] Shores herself produced an edition in response to the deficiencies of the prior editions, though she never published it. Like Krause, her text offers a parallel edition of the Auchinleck and Vernon manuscripts, with the Simeon variants in footnotes. The same year, Judith Perryman submitted an edition based on the Auchinleck alone, using the Vernon to expand the short stanzas and clarify difficult readings. This text was published in 1980, and remains the latest full edition of the poem, despite its being long out of print. In 2003, David Burnley and Alison Wiggins posted a transcription of the Auchinleck text as part of the National Library of Scotland's digital facsimile of the manuscript. Their text of *Tars* follows Perryman's practice of inserting extra lines to complete defective stanzas, but is otherwise a fairly conservative transcription without an apparatus or introduction. This edition follows the policies of the Middle English Texts Series in offering an introduction, a full scholarly apparatus, and explanatory notes to help place the poem in its cultural and historical context for a modern audience.

EDITORIAL STATEMENT

In keeping with the Middle English Texts Series, this edition uses the modern alphabet: thorn (þ) has been expanded to *th* and yogh (ȝ) has been expanded to its closest modern equivalent, usually *y, g,* or *gh*. To ease readability, abbreviations are silently expanded, *i/j* and *u/v* have been normalized according to modern use, an accent has been added to final *-e* when it carries full syllabic value, and *the* has been silently emended to *thee* to distinguish the second person pronoun from the article. Double *ff*'s have been silently emended to single *f*, except for words such as *off*. Capitalization and punctuation are, of course, editorial. There are a few places where the Auchinleck manuscript's text is defective; missing lines have been supplied from the Vernon and are identified in the notes.

---

[84] "*The King of Tars*: A New Edition," ed. Shores, pp. 1–2; she also notes that "they have historical interest, but are of limited usefulness today" (p. 2).

[85] Krause was the first editor to include variants from the Simeon manuscript in his apparatus. In fairness to Warton and Ritson, the Simeon manuscript did not come to the British Library until after their publications.

[86] "*The King of Tars*: A New Edition," ed. Shores, pp. 2–8.

[87] Geist related his opinion to Shores in private correspondence; see "*The King of Tars*: A New Edition," ed. Shores, pp. 6–7.

MANUSCRIPTS

Indexed as item 1108 in Boffey and Edwards, eds., *New Index of Middle English Verse*:
- A: Edinburgh, National Library of Scotland, Advocates' 19.2.1, fols. 7ra–13vb. [Base-text for this edition.]
- V: Oxford, Bodleian Library, Eng.poet.a.1, fols. 304vb–307ra.
- S: London, British Library, Additional 22283, fols. 126rc–128va.

EDITIONS

Ed. Thomas Warton. In *The History of English Poetry, from the Close of the Eleventh to the Commencement of the Eighteenth Century*. 3 vols. London: J. Dodsley; J. Walter; T. Becket; J. Robson; G. Robinson, and J. Bew, 1774. 1.190–97. [Excerpts only]

Ed. Joseph Ritson as "The Kyng of Tars; and the Soudan of Dammas." In *Ancient Engleish Metrical Romanceës*. 2 vols. London: W. Bulmer and Company, 1802. 2.156–203.

Ed. F. Krause as "Kleine publicationen aus der Auchinleck-hs, IX: *The King of Tars*." *Englische Studien* 11 (1888), 1–62.

Ed. Robert J. Geist as "*The King of Tars*: A Medieval Romance." Ph.D. dissertation. University of Illinois, Urbana-Champaign, 1940.

Ed. Doris Shores as "*The King of Tars*: A New Edition." Ph.D. dissertation, New York University, 1969.

Ed. Judith Perryman as *The King of Tars: Ed. from the Auchinleck MS, Advocates 19.2.1*. Heidelberg: Carl Winter, 1980.

Ed. David Burnley and Alison Wiggins. National Library of Scotland. 5 July 2003. Online at http://auchinleck.nls.uk/. [A transcription of the Auchinleck manuscript, the text corrects some obvious errors and follows Perryman's practice of supplying extra lines not in the Auchinleck to repair faults in the meter.]

THE KING OF TARS

Herkneth to me bothe eld and ying, *Listen; old and young*
For Marie's love, that swete thing, *person*
 Al hou a wer bigan *how; war*
Bituene a trewe Cristen king *Between*
5 And an hethen heye lording, *high*
 Of Dames the soudan. *Damascus; sultan*
The king of Tars hadde a wive, *wife*
Feirer might non ben olive — *Fairer; alive*
 That ani wight telle can. *man*
10 A douhter thai hadde hem bituen, *daughter*
Non feirer woman might ben — *No fairer*
 As white as fether of swan. *as [the] feather*

The meiden was schast and blithe of chere *chaste; happy in appearance*
With rode red so blosme on brere *complexion as red as; briar*
15 And eyghen stepe and gray. *eyes shining*
With lowe scholders and white swere *lovely shoulders; neck*
Hir for to sen was gret preier *see; entreaty*
 Of princes proud and play. *playful*
The los of hir gan spring wide *fame; began [to]*
20 In other londes bi ich a side, *on every side*
 So the soudan herd it say. *sultan*
Him thought his hert it brast ofive *[would] burst into five [pieces]*
Bot yif he might have hir to wive *But if (Unless); marry*
 That was so feir a may. *maiden*

25 His messangers he gan calle
And bad hem wightly wenden alle *them all go swiftly*
 To hir fader the king, *father*
And seyd he wald hou so it bifalle *said howsoever it came about*
His douhter clothe in riche palle *fine cloth*
30 And spouse hir with his ring; *spouse (wed)*
And yif he nold, withouten feyl, *if he would not; fail*
He wald hir win in batayl *would; battle*
 With mani an heye lording. *powerful*
The messangers forth thai went

35   To dou the soudan's comandment   *delay*
            Withouten ani duelling.

        Than the king of Tars this understode   *When*
        Almest for wrethe he wex ner wode   *wrath he waxed (grew); mad*
            And seyd thus in sawe: *speech*
40   "Bi Him that dyed on the rode,   *rood (cross)*
        Ich wald arst spille min hert blode   *I would rather; my*
            In bateyl to ben yslawe.   *slain*
        Y nold hir give a Sarazin   *I would not; Saracen*
        For alle the lond that is mine.   *land*
45   The devel him arst to drawe,   *sooner; get*
        Bot sche wil with hir gode wille   *Unless; through*
        Be wedded to him, hirselve to spille.   *destroy*
            Hir thoughtes nought Y no knawe,   *[Of] her; nothing; know*

        "Ac Y schal wite ar than ye pas."   *But; know before*
50   His douhter anon was brought in plas   *[that] place*
            And he axed hir bilive.   *asked her right away*
        "Douhter, the soudan of Damas   *Damascus*
        Yernes for to se thi fas   *Yearns; see; face*
            And wald thee have to wive.   *would*
55   Waldestow, douhter, for tresour   *Would you*
        Forsake Jhesus our Saveour
            That suffred woundes five?"
        The maiden answerd with mild mod   *mood*
        Biforn hir fader ther sche stode   *where*
60   "Nay, lord, so mot Y thrive!   *prosper*

        "Jhesu mi Lord in Trinité
        Lat me never that day yse   *see*
            A tirant for to take.   *tyrant*
        O God and Persones Thre   *One*
65   For Marie love, Thi moder fre,   *noble*
            Gif him arst tene and wrake."   *Give; first suffering; injury*
        The king seyd, "Douhter, be stille.
        Thou schalt never be wedded him tille   *to him*
            For no bost he can make.   *Regardless of any boast*
70   Y schal him sende word ogein   *again*
        That alle his thoughtes ben in vein,   *are*
            For thou hast him forsake."   *refused*

        Right be the self messangers   *by the same*
        That com fro the soudan fers   *fierce*
75   This wordes he him sent: *These words (This message)*
        That sche leved nought on his maners,   *believed; in his religious practices*
        Sche nold nought leten hir preiers   *abandon*

        To God omnipotent.
    He bad him tak another thought,
80   For of his douhter no tit him nought   *he is not obliged*
        For tresore no for rent.   *rent*
    The messangers herd him thus seyn;
    With that word thai turned ogain
        And to the soudan thai went.

85   As the soudan sat at his des,   *on his dais*
    Yserved of the first mes,   *course (mess, meal)*
        Thai com into the halle.
    Bifor tho princes prout in pres   *valiant in battle*
    Her tale to telle withouten les   *Their; falsehood*
90   On knes thai gun doun falle.   *they fell down*
    Thai seyd, "Sir, the king of Tars
    Of wicked wordes is nought scars.   *sparing*
        'Hethen hounde' he gan thee calle;
    And ar he give his douhter thee tille,   *before; to you*
95   Thine hert blod he will spille,
        And thine barouns alle."

    When the soudan this wordes herd   *these*
    Also a wilde bore he ferd.   *As; behaved*
        His robe he rent adoun;   *tore apart*
100   His here he rent of heved and berd;   *hair; from head and beard*
    He schuld venge him with his swerd,   *avenge himself*
        He swore bi Seyn Mahoun.
    The table so hetelich he smot   *violently he struck*
    It fel in to the flore fot-hot   *immediately*
105   And loked as a lyoun.   *[he] appeared to be*
    Al that he raught he smot doun right —   *touched*
    Serjaunt, squier, clerk, and knight,   *Servant*
        Bothe erl and baroun.

    Al thus the soudan ferd, yplight;   *behaved, indeed*
110   Al that day and alle that night
        No man might him schast.   *control*
    Amorwe when it was light,   *The next day (On the morrow)*
    His messangers he sent ful right
    For his barouns wel fast
115   That thai com to his parlement
    Forto heren his jugement,   *To*
        Bothe lest and mast.   *Both the least and the most (greatest)*
    When the parlement was pleyner,   *complete*
    Tho bispac the soudan fer   *Then announced; fierce*
120   And seyd to hem in hast: *them*

"Lordings," he seyd, "what to red.   *advise*
Me hath ben don a gret misdede   *[To] me has; offense*
   Of Tars the Cristen king!   *By*
Y bede him bothe lond and lede   *offered; people*
125 For his douhter worthliche in wede   *esteemed*
   To han wed hir with ring,
And he me sent word ogain
In bateyl Y schuld arst be sleyn   *sooner*
   And mani an heye lording!
130 And certes he schal be forsworn.   *certainly; proven wrong*
Wrotherhele than was he been   *[To] misfortune; born*
   Bot Y therto it bring.   *[will] bring it (calamity) to him*

"And therfore ich have after you sent
And asembled herer this parlement   *here*
135   To wite your conseyle."   *know*
And alle thai seyd with gode entent
Thai were at his comandment,
   Certeyn withouten feile.   *fail*
Right bi that day a fourtennight   *fortnight*
140 Thai schul ben alle redi dight   *prepared*
   With helme, hauberk of meile.   *chain mail*
And whan thai were so at his hest   *command*
The soudan made a riche fest   *feast*
   For love of his bateyle.   *army*

145 The soudan gaderd a rout unride   *gathered a gigantic company*
Of Sarrazins of michel pride   *Saracens; great*
   Opon the king to wende.   *Against; go*
The king of Tars herd that tide;   *news*
He gadred his ost bi ich a side,   *host (army) on every side*
150   Al that he might ofsende.   *summon*
Than bigan wretthe to wake   *wrath*
For that mariage might nought take   *take [place]*
   Of that maiden hende.   *pleasant (gentle; well bred)*
Of bateyl thai gun sett a day,
155 Of Seynt Eline the thridde in May,   *Helen*
   No lenger no wald thai lende.   *desire; delay*

The soudan com with his pouwer   *power (i.e., military force)*
With bright armour and brod baner,
   Into the feld to fight
160 With sexti thousend Sarrazins fer,   *sixty; fierce*
That alle the feldes fer and ner   *[So] that; fields far and near*
   With helmes lemed light.   *shone*
The king of Tars com with his ost,   *host*
With gret pride and michel bost,   *great (many)*

165   With mani an hardi knight,
        And aither ost gan other aseyle.   *either army; assail*
        Ther might men se a strong bateyle   *see*
            That grimli was of sight.   *grim; to behold*

        Ther hewe houndes on Cristen men[1]
170   And feld hem doun bi nighen and ten;   *felled (cut); nine*
            So wilde thai were and wode   *mad*
        That men might sen alle the fen   *bloody mess (see note)*
        Of Cristen both fremd and ken,   *stranger and kin*
            The valays ren on blod.   *ran with*
175   The soudan and his folk that stounde   *moment*
        Hewe adoun with grimli wounde
            Mani a frely fode.   *noble foray*
        Allas, to wele sped Mahoun!   *victory hastened*
        The Cristen men yede al adoun   *suffered defeat*
180   Was nought that hem withstode.   *[There] were none who them (the heathen)*

        The king of Tars seye that sight;   *saw*
        For wretthe he was neye wode, aplight. *wrath; nearly mad, assuredly*
            He hent in hond a spere   *grasped*
        And to the soudan he rode ful right.
185   With a stroke o michel might,   *of great might*
            To grounde he gan him bere.[2]
        Ther he hadde the soudan slawe   *would have; slain*
        Ac ten thousend of hethen lawe   *But; faith*
            Saved him in that were —   *peril*
190   Thai sett him on a ful gode stede
        That was so gode at everi nede
            That no man might him dere.   *harm*

        And when he was opon his stede,
        Him thought he brend so spark on glede[3]
195   For ire and for envie.   *spite*
        He faught so he wald wede: *as if he would go mad*
        Alle that he hit he maked blede.   *bleed*
            "Help, Mahoun!" he gan crie.
        Mani helme ther was ofweved   *struck off*
200   And mani bacinet tocleved   *helmets cut in half*
            And sadles fel emtye;   *saddles fell empty*
        Mani swerd and mani scheld

---

[1] *There [heathen] hounds chopped Christian men [to pieces]*

[2] *He (the king) bore him (the sultan) to the ground, i.e., he unhorsed him*

[3] *It seemed to them that he burned like a spark on a live coal*

And mani knight lay in the feld
    Of Cristen compeynie.

205   The king of Tars seye him so ride   *saw*
    He fleye and durst nought abide   *[That] he fled; dared; linger*
        Homward to his cité
    The Sarrazins folwed in that tide   *followed; time*
    And slough adoun bi ich aside   *cut down on each side*
210   That Cristen folk so fre.   *noble*
    Thritti thousend ther were yslawe   *thirty*
    Of knightes of Cristen lawe
        And that was gret pité.
    Amorwe for her bother sake   *both their sakes*
215   Trewes thai gun bituen hem take   *[A] truce; between*
        A moneth and dayes thre.   *month*

    On a day, the king sat in his halle   *One day*
    And made grete diol with alle,   *sadness*
        For his folk were forlore.   *lost*
220   His douhter com clad in palle   *royal cloth*
    Adoun on knes sche gan to falle   *down*
        And seyd with sikeing sore,   *sighing piteous*
    "Sir, lete me be the soudan's wiif   *wife*
    And rere na more cuntek no striif   *raise; violence nor strife*
225   As hath ben here bifore.
    For me hath mani man ben schent,   *killed*
    Cités nomen and tounes brent;   *taken; towns*
        Allas that ich was bore!   *I was born*

    "Fader, Y wil serve at wille   *willingly*
230   The soudan, bothe loude and stille,   *under all circumstances*
        And leve on God almight,   *[still] believe in*
    Bot it so be, he schal thee spille,   *Since otherwise; kill*
    And alle thi lond take him tille   *take for himself*
        With bateyle and with fight.   *battle*
235   Certes Y nil no lenger dreye   *Certainly I will no longer endure*
    That Cristen folk for me dye —
        It were a diolful sight!"   *doleful (sad)*
    The king of Tars answerd tho,   *then*
    As man that was in sorwe and wo,   *sorrow*
240   Unto that bird bright: *beautiful woman*

    "Now douhter, blisced mot thou be   *blessed must*
    Of Jhesu Crist in Trinité
        The time that thou were bore.   *born*
    For thou wilt save thi moder and me,   *Because*
245   Al thi preier graunt Y thee,   *prayers (entreaties) grant*

Astow hast seyd bifore."   *As you*
"Fader," sche seyd withouten duelling,   *without delay*
"For Jhesu's love, Heven king,
      Yif it thi wille wore,   *were*
250   Do now swithe that Y war there[1]
Ar ani more sorwe arere   *Before; arise*
      That ye be nought forlore."   *lost (forlorn)*

The king of Tars with gode entent   *good*
Hastilich after his wiif he sent,   *Quickly*
255   That levedi that was so hende.   *lady who; gracious*
When sche was comen in present
He seyd, "Dame, our douhter hath ment   *intends*
      To the soudan to wende.
Do loke what rede is now at thee,   *Look; advice*
260   For now er here bot we thre   *are*
      To save Cristen kende."   *people*
The quene answerd withouten feile
"Y no schal never therto conseyle   *I shall never thus advise*
      Our douhter forto schende."   *put to shame*

265   The maiden was ful of sorwe and wo.
"Merci," sche crid hir moder tho   *then*
      With a wel reweful steven.   *piteous voice*
"Moder, it is nought long ago
For me were slawe knightes thro,   *slain; excellent*
270   Thritti thousende and seven.
Forthi Y wil suffre no lenger thrawe   *Therefore; no more*
That Cristen folk be for me slawe,
      With the grace of God in Heven."
Thus, the maiden with wordes stille   *calm*
275   Brought hem bothe in better wille   *disposition*
      With resoun right and even.   *true and impartial*

And when thai were thus at on,   *in agreement*
Messangers thai sent anon
      Unto that riche soudan,   *powerful*
280   To make his frende that were his fon;   *foes*
And for he schuld his men nought slou,   *slay*
      His douhter he graunt him than.
The messangers nold no leng abide;   *would no longer delay*
To the soudan thai went that tide   *hour*
285   And thus thai tel him gan.   *began*
When tho letters weren yradde,   *those; read*

---

[1] *Arrange things quickly so that I will be there (with the sultan)*

The soudan was bothe blithe and glad,   *happy*
    And so was mani a man.

So glad he was in al maners   *in every respect*
290 He cleped to him of his pers   *called to himself; peers*
    Doukes, princes, and kinges.
Into a chaumber thai went yfers   *together*
To dight unto the messangers   *prepare for*
    Gode stones and riche ringes.
295 Bi conseyl of the lordinges alle,
The soudan dede bring into the halle
    Giftes and riche thinges,
And gaf to hem grete plenté,   *gave; great plenty*
To the messangers, with hert fre   *generous heart*
300   And thonked hem her tidinges.   *[for] their news*

And seyd he was alle at his wille,[1]
Arliche and late, loude and stille,   *Early*
    To helpe him at his nede;
No more folk nold he spille.   *would not*
                                                                  to
305 The messangers went the king tille   *action*
    And told him of that dede.
The king and the quene also
Bothen hem was wele and wo,   *Both of them were glad and sad*
    In rime also we rede.   *poem (rhyme) as*
                                                                  lie
310 Gret joie thai hadde withouten les
For that the soudan wald have pes   *peace*
    On Cristen felawerede.   *company*

The first day of Julii tide,   *arrived*
The soudan nold no leng abide;   *would no longer wait*
315   To the king of Tars he sent
Knightes fele and michel pride   *Many knights; great*
And riche jewels is nought to hide
    To gif to his present.   *as his gift*
The messangers, withouten duelling,
320 Com to Tars bifor the king   *your*
    To have his douhter gent.   *noble (gentle)*
Thai welcomed hem with glad chere —   *appearance (cheer)*
Of gret pité now may ye here —
    To chaumber when thai went.

325 Thai maden cri and michel wo   *They made; much*
For thai schuld her douhter forgo   *their daughter lose*

---

[1] *And [the messengers] said he (the sultan of Damascus) was all at his (the king of Tars's) will*

And to the soudan hir sende.
The maiden preyd hem bothe tho   *then*
That thai schuld bi her conseyl do,   *act according to her advice (counsel)*
330   To saven Cristen kende.
"For Y wil suffre no lenger thrawe   *a space of time*
That Cristen folk be for me slawe."
To halle thai gun wende   *began to wind (go)*
And welcomed tho messangers   *those*
335   That com fro the soudan fers   *fierce*
With wordes fre and hende.   *noble and courteous*

Than seyd the quen to hem than,
"Hou fareth your lord, the soudan,   *How fares*
That is so noble a knight?"
340   The messangers answere gan   *did answer*
"He farth as wele as ani man,
And is your frende aplight."   *in truth*
The quen seyd with milde chere,   *humble countenance*
"Wele better thei mi douhter were,   *through*
345   Bi Jhesu ful of might.
Mi douhter is noght to him to gode;
Y vouchesave on him mi blode,   *promise (vouchsafe)*
Thei sche were ten so bright."[1]

The messangers dight hem swithe   *prepared themselves quickly*
350   With knightes fele and stedes stithe   *strong (powerful) horses*
And brought hir into chare.   *[a] chariot*
The king and the quen were unblithe,   *unhappy*
Her sorwe couthe thai no man kithe   *Their; could; reveal*
When thai seye hir forth fare.   *saw her come forth (see t-note)*
355   Into chaumber thai went tho   *then*
When thai were togider bothe to   *two*
Than wakened alle her care.   *awoke; their concern*

The king was in sorwe bounde;   *in sorrow bound*
The quen swoned mani a stounde   *swooned; time*
360   For her douhter dere.   *their*
Knightes and levedis ther hem founde   *ladies*
And tok hem up hole and sounde,   *took*
And comfort hem in fere.   *company*
Thus the quen and the king
365   Lived in sorwe and care, morning;   *mourning*
Great diol it was to here.   *sadness (dole); hear*
Her care was ever aliche newe,   *Their; perpetually*

---

[1] *Even if she were ten [times] as beautiful (virtuous)*

Hem chaunged bothe hide and hewe[1]
   For sorwe and reweli chere.   *pitiful mood*

370   Nou late we ben alle her morning,   *Now let us leave all their mourning*
   And telle we of that maiden ying   *young*
      That to the soudan is fare.   *has gone*
   He com with mani gret lording
   Forto welcome that swete thing   *To*
375   When sche was brought in chare.
   He kist hir wel mani a sithe;   *time*
   His joie couthe he no man kithe —   *could; describe*
      Oway was alle his care.   *Away*
   Into chaumber sche was ladde,   *led*
380   And richeliche sche was cladde   *richly; dressed*
      As hethen wiman ware.   *women were*

   Whan sche was cladde in riche palle,
   The soudan dede his knightes calle
      And badde that maiden forth fett.   *bade; fetch*
385   And when sche com into the halle,
   Bifor the heyghe lordinges alle,   *high*
      Toforn the soudan thai hir sett.   *Before; placed her*
   Gret diol it was forto se,   *sadness; to see*
   The bird that was so bright on ble   *woman; radiant of complexion*
390   To have so foule a mett.   *mate*
   Thei that sche made gret solas   *Although; [appeared to] enjoy herself*
   The sorwe that at hir hert was
      No might it noman lett.   *prevent*

   And whan it was comen to night,
395   The levedi that was so feir and bright,   *lady*
      To chaumber sche gan wende.   *went*
   And therin anon Y you plight,   *promise*
   A riche bed ther was ydight   *prepared*
      Unto that levedi hende.   *gracious*
400   The levedi was to bed ybrought;
   The soudan wild com therin nought   *would*
      Noither for fo no frende —   *foe nor*
   For nothing wold he neyghe that may   *approach; maid*
   Til that sche leved opon his lay,   *believed; law*
405   That was of Cristen kende.   *[She] that*

   Wel lothe war a Cristen man   *loath were*
   To wedde an hethen woman

---

[1] *[Their sadness] changed them both complexion and hue (i.e., their entire appearance changed)*

That leved on fals lawe;   *believed in*
Als loth was that soudan
410   To wed a Cristen woman,
      As Y finde in mi sawe.   *source (story)*
The soudan yede to bed al prest,   *went; immediately*
Knightes and levedis yede to rest;   *went*
      The pople hem gan withdrawe.
415   That miri maiden litel slepe,   *beautiful*
Bot al night wel sore sche wepe   *But*
      Til the day gan dawe.   *began [to] dawn*

And als sche fel on slepe thore   *as; there*
Her thought ther stode hir bifore   *It seemed to her*
420   An hundred houndes blake,   *black*
And bark on hir lasse and more.   *at her all together*
And on ther was that greved hir sore,   *one*
      Oway that wald hir take.   *would*
And sche no durst him nought smite   *dared not; strike*
425   For drede that he wald hir bite,
      Swiche maistri he gan to make.   *So threateningly; began to behave*
And as sche wald fram hem fle,   *from*
Sche seye ther stond develen thre   *saw; three devils*
      And ich brent as a drake.   *each burned like a dragon*

430   So lothliche thai were al ywrought,   *loathly (ugly); shaped*
And ich in hond a gleive brought,   *spear*
      Sche was aferd ful sore.   *very afraid*
On Jhesu Crist was alle hir thought;
Therfore the fendes derd hir nought;   *fiends harmed*
435   Noither lesse no more.   *Not at all*
Fro the fendes sche passed sounde,
And afterward ther com an hounde
      With browes brod and hore.   *hoary*
Almost he hadde hir drawen adoun
440   Ac thurth Jhesus Cristes passioun   *But through*
      Sche was ysaved thore.   *there*

Yete hir thought withouten lesing   *it seemed to her; lying*
Als sche lay in hir swevening   *swoon*
      (That selcouthe was to rede)   *strange; tell*
445   That blac hounde hir was folweing.
Thurth might of Jhesu, Heven king,   *Through*
      Spac to hir in manhede   *manly demeanor*
In white clothes als a knight,
And seyd to hir, "Mi swete wight,   *lady (person)*
450   No tharf thee nothing drede   *You need not dread anything*
Of Ternagaunt no of Mahoun.

Thi Lord that suffred passioun
    Schal help thee at thi nede."

      And when the maiden was awaked,
455   For drede of that, wel sore sche quaked,   *very forcefully; shook*
      For love of her swevening.   *dream*
    On hir bed sche sat al naked;
    To Jhesu hir preier sche maked,   *made*
      Almightful Heven king.   *Almighty*
460   As wis as He hir dere bought   *certainly; dearly redeemed*
    Of that swevening in slepe sche thought
      Schuld turn to gode ending.   *good*
    And when the maiden risen was
    The riche soudan of Damas
465   To his temple he gan hir bring.

    Than seyd the soudan to that may,   *maiden*
    "Thou most bileve opon mi lay   *law (religion)*
      And knele now here adoun
    And forsake thi fals lay
470   That thou hast leved on mani a day,   *believed in*
      And anour Seyn Mahoun!   *worship Saint*
    And certes, bot thou wilt anon,   *unless*
    Thi fader Y schal with wer slon   *war slay*
      Bi Jovin and Plotoun!   *Jove; Pluto*
475   And bi Mahoun and Ternagant
    Ther schal no man ben his waraunt —   *be his defender*
      Empour no king with croun."

    The maiden answerd with mild chere   *demeanor*
    To the soudan as ye may here:
480   "Sir, Y nil thee nought greve.   *offend*
    Teche me now and lat me here
    Hou Y schal make mi preiere
      When ich on hem bileve.
    To Mahoun ichil me take   *I will commit myself*
485   And Jhesu Crist mi Lord forsake,
      That made Adam and Eve,
    And seththen serve thee at wille   *afterward*
    Arliche and lat, loude and stille,   *Early*
      A morwe and an eve."   *By morning and on evening*

490   Than was the soudan glad and blithe,
    And thanked Mahoun mani sithe   *times*
      That sche was so biknawe.   *converted*
    His joie couthe he no man kithe;   *could he to no man convey*
    He bad hir gon and kis swithe   *go; quickly*

495   Alle thine godes on rawe.
        Sche kist Mahoun and Apolin,
        Astirot and Sir Jovin.
            For drede of wordes awe,
        And while sche was in the temple
500   Of Ternagant and Jubiter,
            Sche lerd the hethen lawe.   *learned*

        And thei sche al the lawes couthe   *though; knew*
        And seyd hem openliche with hir mouthe,
            Jhesu forgat sche nought.
505   Wher that sche was, bi northe or southe,   *by*
        No minstral with harp no crouthe   *musical instrument*
            No might chaunge hir thought.
        The soudan wende night and day   *thought*
        That sche hadde leved opon his lay   *believed; law*
510   Bot al he was bicought,   *deceived*
        For when sche was bi herselveon,
        To Jhesu sche made hir mon,   *prayer*
            That alle this world hath wrought.   *Who*

        The soudan dede cri that tide   *proclaim at that time*
515   Overal bi ich a side   *(i.e., everywhere)*
            A turnament to take
        And duhti men on hors to ride,   *powerful*
        And dubbed hem in that tide
            And knightes gan he make.
520   The trumpes gun forto blowe;
        Knightes priked out o rouwe   *pricked (spurred) in a row*
            On stedes white and blake.
        Ther might men se sone and swithe,   *immediately and quickly*
        Strong men her strengthe kithe   *their; demonstrate*
525   For that maiden sake.

        The Cristen maiden and the soudan
        In the castel leyen than   *stayed*
            The turnament to bihold.
        And tho the turnament bigan,   *when*
530   Ther was samned mani a man   *assembled*
            Of Sarrazins stout and bold.
        To sen ther was a semly sight   *see; pleasant*
        Of thritti thousend of helmes bright   *thirty*
            (In gest as it is told).   *tale*
535   Thai leyden on as thai were wrothe   *mad*
        With swerdes and with maces bothe
            Knightes bothe yong and old.

Wel mani helme ther was ofweved   *struck off*
And mani bacinet tocleved   *helmets split apart*
540   And knightes driven to grounde.
Sum ther fel doun on her heved   *their heads*
And sum in the diche lay todreved   *scattered*
    And siked sore unsounde.   *sighed sorely wounded*
The turnament last tho yplight   *then indeed*
545 Fram the morwe to the night   *morning*
    Of men of michel mounde;   *prowess*
Amorwe the soudan wedded that may   *On the next day; maiden*
In the maner of his lay,
    In gest as it is founde.

550 Atte his bridale was noble fest,
Riche, real, and onest —   *Rich, regal, and seemly*
    Doukes, kinges with croun.   *crown*
For ther was melodi with the mest   *to the highest degree*
Of harp and fithel and of gest   *songs (tales)*
555   To lordinges of renoun.   *For*
Ther was geven to the menstrels
Robes riche and mani juweles   *From*
    Of erl and of baroun.   *fortnight (two weeks)*
The fest lasted fourtenight   *food; in truth*
560 With mete and drink anough, aplight   *abundance*
    Plenté and gret fousoun.

That levedi, so feir and so fre,   *noble*
Was with hir lord bot monethes thre
    Than he gat hir with childe.   *Then*
565 When it was geten, sche chaunged ble;   *appearance*
The soudan himself that gan se —
    Jolif he was and wilde.   *Joyful; beside himself*
Ther while sche was with child, aplight,
Sche bad to Jhesu ful of might
570   Fram schame He schulde hir schilde.
Atte fourti woukes ende   *At forty weeks'*
The levedi was deliverd o bende[1]
    Thurth help of Mari milde.   *Through*

And when the child was ybore,
575 Wel sori wimen were therfore,
    For lim no hadde it non,   *limb*
Bot as a rond of flesche yschore   *round (lump); cut with a sharp instrument*
In chaumber it lay hem bifore

---

[1] *That lady was delivered from confinement in child-bearing*

         Withouten blod and bon.
580   For sorwe the levedi wald dye,   *wished to die*
         For it hadde noither nose no eye
            Bot lay ded as the ston.
         The soudan com to chaumber that tide   *time*
         And with his wiif he gan to chide
585   That wo was hir bigon.   *had begun [with] her*

         "O dame," he seyd biforn,
         "Ogain mi godes thou art forsworn!   *Against*
            With right resoun Y preve   *prove*
         The childe that is here of thee born
590   Bothe lim and lith it is forlorn   *limb; joint*
            Alle thurth thi fals bileve!   *through*
         Thou levest nought wele afine   *thoroughly*
         On Jubiter no on Apoline,   *nor*
            A morwe na an eve,   *[Neither] in the morning nor in the evening*
595   No in Mahoun no in Ternagant.   *Neither; nor*
         Therfore is lorn this litel faunt.   *child*
            No wonder thei me greve!"   *they (i.e., the gods) make me sorry*

         The levedi answerd and seyd tho,
         Ther sche lay in care and wo,   *There*
600   "Leve sir, lat be that thought;   *Honorable*
         The child was geten bitwen ous to.   *begotten; us*
         For thi bileve it farth so,   *fares*
            Bi Him that ous hath wrought!
         Take now this flesche and bere it anon
605   Bifor thine godes everichon   *gods every one*
            That thou no lete it nought,   *So that you spare nothing*
         And pray thine godes al yfere,   *together*
         Astow art hem leve and dere,   *As you are to them beloved and dear*
            To live that it be brought.   *life*

610   "And yif Mahoun and Jovin can
         Make it fourmed after a man
            With liif and limes aright,   *proper*
         Bi Jhesu Crist that this warld wan
         Y schal leve thee better than
615   That thai ar ful of might.
         And bot thai it to live bring   *unless; life*
         Y nil leven on hem nothing
            Noither bi day no night."
         The soudan toke that flesche anon
620   Into his temple he gan to gon
            Ther his godes were dight.   *prepared*

	Biforn his goddes he gan it leyn	
	And held up his honden tuein,	two
	While men might go five mile.[1]	
625	"A, mightful Mahoun," he gan to seyn,	Oh
	"And Ternagaunt, of michel meyn,	might
	In you was never no gile.	
	Seyn Jubiter and Apolin,	Saint
	Astirot and Seyn Jovin,	Astarte (Venus)
630	Help now in this perile."	disaster
	Oft he kneled and oft he ros	rose
	And crid so long til he was hos	hoarse
	And al he tint his while.	wasted his time

	And when he hadde al ypreyd,	
635	And alle that ever he couthe he seyd,	could
	The flesche lay stille as ston.	
	Anon he stert up at a breyd,	suddenly (in a moment)
	And in his hert he was atreyd,	troubled
	For lim no hadde it non.	limb
640	He biheld on his godes alle	looked upon
	And seye ther might no bot bifalle;	saw; no help come
	Wel wo was him bigon.	very deeply grieved was he
	"O Sir Mahoun," he gan to grede,	cry out
	"Wil ye nought helpe me at this nede?	
645	The devel you brenne ichon!"	burn each one [of] you

	He hent a staf with grete hete	lifted; vehemence
	And stirt anon his godes to bete	started
	And drough hem alle adoun,	pulled them
	And leyd on til he gan to swete	
650	And gaf hem strokes gode and gret,	gave the
	Both Jovine and Plotoun.	
	And alder best he bete afin	best of all; thoroughly
	Jubiter and Apolin,	
	And brac hem arm and croun,	broke
655	And Ternagaunt that was her brother —	their
	He no lete never a lime with other	left; limb
	No of his god Mahoun.	Nor

	And when he hadde beten hem gode won	very well
	Yete lay the flesche stille so ston,	
660	An heye on his auter.	On high; altar
	He tok it in his hond anon	
	And into chaumber he gan gon,	began to go

---

[1] *For as long as it would take one to walk five miles*

And seyd, "Lo, have it here.
Ich have don al that Y can

665   To make it fourmed after a man   *like*
With kneleing and preier,
And for alle that ichave hem bisought   *I have*
Mine godes no may help me nought.
The devel hem sett afere!"   *them; afire*

670   And than answerd that gode wiman   *woman*
Wel hendeliche to that soudan: *courteously*
"Leve sir, here mi speche.   *Beloved; hear*
The best rede that Y can,   *advice; know*
Bi Jhesu Crist that made man,

675   Now ichil you teche.   *I shall teach you*
Now thou hast proved god thine,   *your gods*
Yif me leve to asay mine   *Give; test*
Whether is better leche.   *physician*
And, leve sir, prey thee this: *dear*

680   Leve on Him that stronger is   *Believe*
For doute of more wreche."   *fear; affliction*

The soudan answerd hir thore.   *there (then)*
In hert he was agreved sore,
To sen that selcouthe sight.   *see; strange*

685   "Now, dame, ichil do bi thi lore.   *act according to your teaching*
Yif that Y may se bifore   *If*
Thi God is of swiche might   *such*
With ani vertu that He can   *virtue*
Make it fourmed after a man,

690   With liif and limes aright,
Alle mi godes ichil forsake
And to Jhesu thi Lord me take,
As icham gentil knight."   *As I am [a]*

Wel blithe was the levedi than   *pleased; lady then*

695   For that hir lord the riche soudan
Hadde graunted hir preier.
For hope he schuld be Cristen man,
Sche thonked Him that this world wan
And Mari His moder dere.

700   Now ginneth here a miri pas   *merry interlude*
Hou that child ycristned was   *How*
With limes al hole and fere,   *capable (healthy)*
And hou the soudan of Damas
Was cristned for that ich cas —   *very reason*

705   Now herken and ye may here.   *listen (hearken)*

Than seyd the levedi in that stounde,   *occasion*
"Thou hast in thi prisoun bounde
        Mani a Cristen man.
Do seche overalle bi loft and grounde;   *seek (i.e., high and low)*
710   Yif ani Cristen prest be founde,
        Bring him bifor me than
And Y schal ar tomorwe at none   *before; noon*
Wite what Jhesu Crist can done   *Know for a fact that*
        More than thine maumettes can."   *idols*
715   Anon the prisouns weren ysought;   *Soon*
Thai founden a prest and forth him brought
        Bi hest of that soudan.   *command*

He com bifore that levedi fre,
And gret hir feir opon his kne,   *greeted*
720   And seyd with sikeing sore,   *sighing*
"Madame, yblisced mot thou be   *blessed must*
Of Jhesu Crist in Trinité
        That of Mari was bore."
The levedi seyd, "Artw a prest?   *Are you*
725   Tel me sothe yif that tow best.   *truly if you are*
        Canstow of Cristen lore?"   *Do you know*
"Madame," seyd the prest anon,
"*In verbo Dei* ich was on,   *By the word of God; one*
        Tuenti winter gon and more.   *Twenty winters ago*

730   "Ac dame," he seyd, "bi Seyn Jon,   *But; Saint*
Ten winter song Y masse non   *sang*
        And that me liketh ille.   *I didn't like*
For so long it is now gon   *it has now been*
Ichave ben in thi prisoun of ston   *I have been*
735   With wrong and gret unskille."   *very unjustly*
The levedi seyd, "Lat be thi fare.   *Cease your excuses*
Thou schalt be brought out of thi care
        And tow wilt held thee stille.   *If you will be quiet*
For thurth thine help in this stounde,   *moment*
740   We schul make Cristen men of houndes —   *heathens*
        God graunt it yif it be His wille."

Than seyd the soudan's wiif,
"Thou most do stille withouten striif   *quietly*
        A wel gret priveté.   *mystery (see t-note)*
745   Hali water thou most make,   *Holy*
And this ich flesche thou take,   *very*
        Al for the love of me,
And cristen it withouten blame   *baptize*

	In the worthschipe of the Fader's name	*honor (worship)*
750	That sitt in Trinité.	

"For in Him is mine hope aplight,   *indeed*
The Fader that is ful of might
   Mi sorwe schal me slake.
Yif it were cristned aright,   *properly*
755 It schuld have fourme to se bi sight
   With lim and liif to wake."   *to stir [into life]*
That levedi comand anon   *commanded*
Hir maidens out of chaumber gon   *go*
   For dred of wraying sake.   *the sin of betrayal*
760 The prest no leng nold abide;   *no longer would*
A feir vessel he tok that tide
   And hali water he gan make.   *made*

At missomer tide that ded was don   *midsummer; deed*
Thurth help of God that sitt in trone,
765   As Y you tel may.
The prest toke the flesche anon   *took*
And cleped it the name of Jon   *hailed it [by]*
   In worthschip of the day.   *worship (honor)*
And when that it cristned was
770 It hadde liif and lim and fas   *life; limb; face*
   And crid with gret deray,   *cried; great commotion*
And hadde hide and flesche and fel   *skin*
And alle that ever therto bifel,   *to this happened*
   In gest as Y you say.   *story*

775 Feirer child might non be bore —
It no hadde never a lime forlore,   *had never; lost*
   Wele schapen it was, withalle;   *moreover*
The prest no lenge duelled thore   *longer stayed there*
And yede and teld the soudan fore   *But went forth*
780   Ther he was in the halle.   *Where*
That levedi ther sche lay in bed
That richeliche was bischred   *covered over*
   With gold and purpel palle.
The child sche take to hir blive   *took; quickly*
785 And thonked our levedi with joies five
   The feir grace ther was bifalle.

And seyd, "Lord, ich pray Thee,
Almighti God in Trinité,
   So give me might and space   *So [to]*
790 That Y may that day yse
Mi lord wald ycristned be,   *would*

The soudan of Damas."
Than cam the soudan that was blac,
And sche schewed him the child and spac   *spoke*
795   With liif and limes and face.
Sche seyd, "Mahoun no Apolin   *[Neither] Mohammed nor Apollo*
Is nought worth the brostle of a swin   *bristle; pig*
        Ogain mi Lordes grace!"   *Against (Compared to)*

The soudan seyd, "Leman min,   *Sweetheart*
800   Ywis icham glad afin   *Indeed; thoroughly*
        Of this child that Y se."
"Ya, sir, bi Seyn Martin   *Saint*
Yif the halvendel wer thin   *half*
        Wel glad might thou be."
805   "O dame," he seyd, "how is that?
Is it nought min that Y bigat?"
        "No, sir," than seyd sche,
"Bot thou were cristned so it is —   *Unless; as it (the child) is*
Thou no hast no part theron ywis,   *have no*
810   Noither of the child ne of me.   *nor*

"And bot thou wilt Mahoun forsake   *unless*
And to Jhesu mi Lord thee take,
        That tholed woundes five —   *suffered*
Anon thou do thee Cristen make —
815   Thou might be ferd for sorwe and wrake   *afraid; injury*
        While that thou art olive.   *alive*
And yif thou were a Cristen man
Bothe weren thine," sche seyd than,   *were*
        "Thi childe and eke thi wive.   *also*
820   When thou art dede, thou schalt wende   *dead; go*
Into blis withouten ende,
        Thi joie may no man kithe."   *know*

The soudan seye wele bi sight   *saw*
That Jhesu was of more might
825   Than was his fals lawe.
He seyd, "Dame, anon right
Ichil forsake mi god aplight —   *gods*
        Thai schal be brent and drawe.   *burned*
Ac telle me now par charité,   *for the love of God*
830   And for the love thou has to me,
        What schal Y seyn in sawe?   *What shall I say*
Now ichave forsaken mi lay.   *law (religion)*
Tel me now what is your fay,   *faith (religion)*
        And ichil lere wel fawe."   *eagerly*

835 Than seyd that levedi hende and fre,
     "Understond, sir, par charité,
        On Jhesu Cristes lay: *law*
     Hou He was and ever schal be
     O God and Persones Thre,
840   And light in Mari that may,   *alit; maiden*
     And in hir bodi nam flesche and blod,   *became*
     And hou He bought ous on the rode,   *redeemed; rood (cross)*
        Opon the Gode Friday;
     And hou His gost went to Helle   *spirit*
845 Satanas pousté for to felle   *To vanquish Satan's power*
        And brought mankin oway.   *mankind away*

     "The thridde day in the morning
     To live He ros withouten lesing   *lying*
        As He com of the rode,   *off the cross*
850 And gaf His frendes comforting
     And steye to Heven as mightful king   *ascended*
        Bothe with flesche and blod.
     As it is founden in holy writ,
     On His Fader right hond He sitt,   *Father's*
855   And is wel mild of mode;   *mild of disposition*
     As it is writen in the crede,
     He demeth bothe the quic and ded   *judges; living*
        The feble and eke the gode.   *[morally] weak; also*

     "And al this warld schal todrive,   *world; scatter*
860 And man arise fram ded to live,
        Right dome to understond.   *judgment; receive*
     And than schal Jhesu, withouten strive,   *strife*
     Schewe His blodi woundes five   *Show*
        That He for ous gan fond.   *experienced*
865 And than schal He withouten mis   *error*
     Deme ich man after he is,   *Judge each man according to his deeds*
        Erl, baroun, and bond.   *bondsman*
     Leve heron," sche seyd than,   *Believe in this*
     "And do thee make a Cristen man   *become*
870   For no thing thou no wond."   *delay*

     Than seyd the soudan, "Dame, be stille.
     Y schal be cristned thurth Godes wille   *through*
        Ar than the thridde day.   *Before*
     Loth me were mi soule to spille.   *I would be loath; destroy*
875 Preye now the prest, he com ous tille   *to us*
        And teche me Cristen lay
     As priveliche as it may be.
     That no man wite bot we thre   *secretly (privately)*
                                                      knows (witness)

	Als forth as ye may.	*So far as*
880	And ani it wist heye or lowe,	*If; knew*
	Thou schalt be brent and Y todrawe	*drawn*
	And we forsoke our fay."	

Anon the prest answerd than
Hendeliche to that soudan   *Graciously*
885   "Sir, icham redi here
With alle the pouwer that Y can   *know*
For to make thee Cristen man
  And Godes lay to lere."   *law to learn*
His hond opon his brest he leyd,   *his (i.e., the sultan's) breast*
890   "In verbo Dei," he swore and seyd,   *By the word of God*
  "Unto you bothe yfere,   *together*
Wel trewe and trusti schal Y be
With alle that ever falleth to me
  To help with mi pouwere."

895   Amorwe, when the prest gan wake,   *The next day*
A wel feir fessel he gan take   *vessel*
  With water clere and cold,
And halwed it for the soudan sake   *sanctified; sultan's*
And his preier he gan make
900   To Jhesu that Judas sold
And to Marie, His moder dere,
Tho that the soudan cristned were,   *Then*
  That was so stout and bold,
He schuld gif him might and space   *(i.e., Christ should give the sultan)*
905   Thurth his vertu and his grace   *Through*
  His cristendom wele to hold.   *christian faith*

And when it was light of day
The riche soudan ther he lay   *mighty; [from] where*
  Up bigan to arise.
910   To the prest he went his way
And halp him alle that he may   *help*
  That fel to his servise.
And when the prest hadde tho   *then*
Dight redi that fel therto   *Prepared [everything] that appertained to this*
915   In al maner wise,
The soudan with gode wille anon
Dede off his clothes everichon   *Took*
  To reseyve his baptize.   *baptism*

The Cristen prest hight Cleophas;   *was called*
920   He cleped the soudan of Damas   *named*
  After his owhen name.   *own*

His hide that blac and lothely was   *loathly*
Al white bicom thurth Godes gras   *through; grace*
   And clere withouten blame.
925   And when the soudan seye that sight,   *saw*
Than leved he wele on God almight;   *believed*
   His care went to game.   *turned into mirth*
And when the prest hadde alle yseyd   *pronounced (said)*
And haly water on him leyd,
930   To chaumber thai went ysame.   *together*

When he com ther the levedi lay,   *where*
"Lo, dame," he gan to say,
   "Certeyne, thi God is trewe."
The levedi thonked God that day;
935   For joie sche wepe with eyghen gray,   *eyes*
   Unnethe hir lord sche knewe.
Than wist sche wele in hir thought   *knew*
That on Mahoun leved he nought
   For chaunged was his hewe.   *changed*
940   For that hir lord was cristned so,
Oway was went al hir wo —
   Hir joie gan wax al newe.   *began [to] increase anew*

"Mi lord," sche seyd with hert fre,
"Sende now this prest in priveté   *secret*
945   To mi fader the king,
And pray him for the love of me
That he com swithe hider to thee   *swiftly here*
   With alle that he may bring.
And when mi fader is to thee come,
950   Do cristen thi lond alle and some,   *christen (baptize)*
   Bothe eld and ying.
And he that wil be cristned nought,
Loke to the deth that he be brought,
   Withouten ani duelleing."   *delay*

955   The soudan tok the prest bi hond   *by [the] hand*
And bad him wende and nought no wond   *go without hesitation*
   To the king of Tars ful gare,
And do him al to understond
Hou Jhesu Crist thurth His sond   *through; message*
960   Hath brought hem out of care,
And bid him bring with him his ost   *host*
Priveliche withouten bost —   *Secretly*
   For nothing he no spare.
And Cleophas, with gode entent,

965   To do the soudan's comandment
          To Tars he gan fare.   *began to travel*

       And when the prest, Sir Cleophas,
       Com to the court thurth Godes grace   *through*
          Withouten ani duelling,   *delay*
970   He teld the king alle that cas: *told; case*
       Hou the child ded born was,   *dead*
          A misforschapen thing,
       And thurth the preier of his wiif
       Hou God hadde sent it leme and liif   *limbs*
975   In water ate cristening,   *at*
       And hou that hethen soudan
       Was bicome a Cristen man
          Thurth the might of Heven king.   *Through*

       He radde the letter that he brought,[1]
980   And in the letter he fond ywrought —   *written*
          In gest as Y you say —
       Hou that the soudan him bisought
       To com to him and lat it nought   *delay*
          Opon a certeyne day,
985   And bring with him alle his ost   *host (army)*
       To take his lond bi everich cost,   *every*
          And serche in his cuntray;
       Who that wold nought cristned be,
       He schuld be honged opon a tre
990   Withouten ani delay.

       Blither might no man ben.   *Happier*
       He cleped his barouns and the quen   *called*
          And told hem thus in sawe   *saying*
       Hou the soudan stout and kene
995   Was cristned withouten wene   *without a doubt*
          And leved on Cristes lawe,
       "And therfore he hath don sent me bi sond   *sent; messenger*
       He wil do cristen alle his lond   *baptize*
          Yif that he might wel fawe,   *eagerly*
1000   And he that wil nought take cristening,
       No be he never so heye lording,   *Be he never so high (important) a lord*
          He schal hong and drawe.   *shall [be] hung and drawn*

       "And therfore Y pray you now right,
       Erl, baroun, douk, and knight,   *duke*

---

[1] *He (the king of Tars) read the letter that he (Cleophas) brought*

1005	Do alle your folk bide	*bid*
	With helme on heved and brini bright	*head; coat of mail*
	That ye ben alle redi dight	*completely ready*
	To help me at this nede."	
	Thai sent over al bi ich a side	*on every side*
1010	For mani Cristen men that tide	
	That duhti were of dede.	*doughty*
	The king him dight for to wende	*depart*
	With sexti thousende knightes hende	*sixty; skillful*
	That was a feir ferred.	*fair company*
1015	The king com withouten lett	*delay*
	The selve day that him was sett	*very same*
	To the soudan wel gare.	*promptly*
	And when thai were togider mett,	*were together*
	A miri greteing ther was gret	*merry; greeted*
1020	With lordinges lasse and mare.	*lesser and greater*
	Ther was rewthe forto sen	*pity*
	Hou the levedi fel on knen	*lady; knees*
	Biforn hir fader thare;	
	Ther was joie and mirthe also	
1025	To here hem speken of wele and wo	
	Her aventours als thai were.	*Their adventures as*
	The soudan dede his barouns calle	*did*
	And seththen anon his knightes alle	
	And after alle his meyné,	*retainers*
1030	And when thai come into the halle,	
	He seyd, "Hou so it bifalle,	*However*
	Ye mot ycristned be.	*must be baptized*
	Miselven, ich have Mahoun forsake	*Myself, I*
	And Cristendom ich have ytake,	*I have taken Christianity*
1035	And certes so mot ye.	*Must*
	And hye that wil nought so anon	*they; not [do] so*
	Thai schul be heveded erverichon	*beheaded*
	Bi Him that dyed on tre."	*(i.e., the cross)*
	When he hadde thus ytold	
1040	Mani Sarrazin stout and bold	*Saracens*
	That in his court were,	
	Mani seyd that thai wold,	
	And mani seyd that thai nold	*would not*
	Be cristned in non maner.	*no way*
1045	Tho that Mahoun wald forsake,	*would*
	Cristen men he lete hem make	*caused them to be made*
	And were him lef and dere;	*beloved*
	And he that dede nought bi his rede	*not; advice*

	Anon he dede strike off his hed	*head*
1050	Right fast bi the swere.	*neck*
	The soudan had in prisoun dight	*cast*
	Ten thousend Cristen men, yplight,	*indeed*
	Of mani uncouthe thede.	*unknown people*
	He dede hem liver anon right	*did deliver them*
1055	And tho that were strong and wight,	*valiant*
	He gaf hem armour and stede;	*gave; steeds*
	And tho he seye that might nought so,	*those; saw*
	He gaf hem mete and drink therto	
	And alle that hem was nede.	*that they needed*
1060	Ther might men se with that soudan	*see*
	Mani blithe Cristen man,	*happy*
	In gest as so we rede.	
	When he hadde don thus that tide,	*time*
	Over al his lond bi ich aside	*each*
1065	The word wel wide sprong.	
	Five hethen kinges that tide	
	And mani hethen douke unride	*many a savage heathen commander*
	With pople gret and strong	*army great*
	Thai sent aboute ner and fer	*near; far*
1070	Opon that soudan for to wer,	*make war*
	And seyd for that wrong,	
	Bi Mahoun and Ternagaunt,	
	Ther schuld nought ben his warant[1]	
	Bot ben drawe and hong.	
1075	Tho fif kinges of prout parayle	*Those five; of valiant appearance*
	Dight hem redi to that bateyle;	*Prepared themselves; battle*
	Wel stout and strong thai were.	
	Hou the soudan gan hem aseyle	*began to assail them*
	And what thai hete withouten feile,	*are named; fail*
1080	Now herken and ye may here.	*listen; hear*
	King Canadok and King Lesias,	
	King Carmel and King Clamadas,	
	And King Memarok her fere.	*their companions*
	Opon the soudan with wer thai went,	*war*
1085	His men thai slough, his tounes brent	*slew; towns [they] burned*
	With strengthe and gret pouwer.	
	The king of Tars and the soudan,	
	Day of bateyle thai gun tan	*began to set*

---

[1] *There should be no protector for him*

Ogein tho kinges five.   *those*
1090 Ac ever ogein a Cristen man,   *But; against*
Ten hethen houndes wer than
Of Sarrazins stout and stithe.   *proud and powerful*
Now herkneth to me bothe old and ying
Hou the soudan and the king
1095 Amonges hem gun drive,   *began [to] drive*
And hou the Sarrazins that day
Opped hevedles for her pay —   *Hopped headless; their reward*
Now listen and ye may lithe.   *hear*

The Cristen soudan that tide   *time*
1100 Toke a spere and gan to ride
To Canadok that was kene.   *Against; bold*
And Canadok with gret pride,
With a spere gan him abide   *did await him*
To wite and nought atwene.   *punish without delay*
1105 So hard thai driven togider there
That her launces bothe yfere   *together*
Brosten hem bituene.   *Burst between them*
The soudan drough his fauchoun gode   *drew; falchion (curved sword)*
The kinges heved with alle the hode   *head*
1110 He strok off quite and clene.   *struck; completely*

King Lesias of Tabarie
To the soudan he gan heye,   *began to hurry*
For Canadok his felawe.   *On behalf of (i.e., to avenge)*
With a spere that was trusti
1115 He rode to the soudan wel an hey   *quickly*
And thought him have yslawe.
The king of Tars bituen hem rod
And Lesias' strok he abod   *withstood*
(As Y finde in mi sawe)   *tale*
1120 And smot him so on the scheld
That top seyl in the feld;   *sailed into the field (see note)*
He made him overthrawe.   *fall down*

He lepe on hors and gan to ride   *leapt*
And slough adoun bi ich aside   *each side*
1125 That he bifor him founde.
Wham that Lesias hit in that tide,   *Whom*
Were he douk or prince o pride,   *duke or prince in pride*
He gaf him dedly wounde.
The king of Tars com with a spere
1130 And thurth his sides he gan it bere   *through*
That ded he fel to grounde.   *dead*
Than sett the Sarrazins up a cri   *raised*

"A, Mahoun, ful of meistri,   *power*
   Help ous in this stounde!"   *moment*

1135 When King Carmel herd that, him was wo;   *he was sorrowful*
    To fight anon he was ful thro.   *eager*
      A spere an hond he hent.   *carried*
    He priked his stede and dede him go.   *spurred; made*
    He thought the king of Tars to slo   *slay*
1140   Er he thennes went.   *Before he went from there*
    He smot the king of Tars that tide   *time*
    Thurth his hauberk a wounde wide   *Through; hauberk armor*
      That neighe he hadde him schent.   *almost; slain*
    The king out of his sadel fel;
1145 The blod out of his wounde gan wel
      That mani man hem biment.   *bemoaned*

    For sorwe the soudan wald wede;   *sorrow; would go mad*
    When he seighe his woundes blede,[1]
      He rode to him with mayn.   *retainers*
1150 He and the Cristen ferred   *company*
    Brought the king of Tars his stede
      And sett him up ogayn.
    And when he was on hors braught
    Alle that ever he araught   *reached*
1155   He clef him to the brayn.   *cleaved*
    King Carmel tho to him went   *through*
    And gaf him swiche another dent   *such*
      That ner he hadde him sleyn.   *nearly*

    And when the soudan that yseighe   *saw*
1160 Al wode he wex for wrethe neye —   *mad; grew; anger nearly*
      He rode to King Carmele.
    He smot him on the helme an heighe   *on high*
    That thurth the breyn it fleighe   *(i.e., his sword) flew*
      That no leche might him hele.   *physician; heal*
1165 King Clamadas com rideing than
    With a glaive to the soudan,
      And thought with him to dele,   *engage*
    And smot him oboven the scheld
    That neighe he feld him in the feld   *nearly*
1170   Among tho houndes fele.   *those many hounds*

    The king of Tars in that stounde
    Hadde spite of that hethen hounde   *strong hatred for*

---

[1] *When he (the sultan) saw his (the king of Tars') wounds bleed*

	That was so stout and beld.	*courageous*
	He swore, "Bi Him that tholed wounde	*suffered*
1175	The dogge schal adoun to grounde	
	That fightes thus in feld."	
	He rode to him anon right	*at once*
	And smot to him a strok of might —	
	Atuo he clef his scheld	*In two; clove*
1180	And thurth his hert the swerd gan glide;	*through*
	The blod ran out bi ich a side	
	And so he him aqueld.	*killed*

	Than was King Memaroc in gret peyn,	
	For his four felawes were sleyn	
1185	And in the feld todreved.	*scattered*
	He priked his stede opon the pleyn	*spurred*
	And fleye oway with might and mayn	*fled*
	For dred to hide his heved.	*head*
	The soudan seyghe him oway ride;	*saw*
1190	He priked after him in that tide,	*rode; time*
	For no thing he it bileved,	
	And smot him so above the scheld	
	That helme and heved fleyghe in the feld	*head flew*
	Ful wightlike off it weved.	*vigorously; severed*

1195	When the Sarrazins seyghen alle	*saw*
	That Memarok was to grounde yfalle	
	And namore up arise,	
	"Allas, Mahoun!" thai gan to calle,	
	"Whi latestow Cristen hewe ous smale?[1]	
1200	Wicke is thi servise!"	*Wicked*
	Thai fleyghe for dred alle yfere	*flew; all together*
	And dreynt hem in o river	*drowned themselves in a river*
	So sore hem gan agrise.	*So greatly afraid of them were they*
	The bateyle last swithe long	*so*
1205	Til it were time of evensong	*evening song*
	Er thai might win the prise.	*Before; victory*

	The Sarrazins flowe bi ich aside;	*fled from each side*
	The Cristen folk after gan ride,	
	And schadde hem breyn and blod.	*shed their*
1210	Ther was non that might him hide	*hide himself*
	That he nas sleyn in that tide	*he was not*
	With fight ogeyn hem stode.	*[Who] with arms against them*
	And tho that yold hem to the pes,	*yielded themselves*

---

[1] *Why do you let the Christians chop us to pieces*

1215	The soudan swore withouten les	*rood (cross)*
	Bi Him that dyed on rode,	*religion (law)*
	He that nold nought forsake his lay,	*forfeit; very*
	He schuld forlesse that ich day	*head (see note)*
	The bal up in the hode.	

	Thritti thousende ther were take	*Thirty*
1220	Of Sarrains bothe blo and blac	*dark and black*
	And don in his prisoun.	*done (placed)*
	And he that wald his lay forsake,	*would*
	Cristen men he lete him make	*them be made*
	With gret devocioun.	
1225	And thai that wald be cristned nought,	
	Into a stede thai weren ybrought	*place*
	A mile withouten the toun	*outside of*
	And Cristen men withouten wene	*doubt*
	Striken off her hevedes al bidene.	*heads all completely*

1230	Thus the ladi with hire lore	*wisdom (see t-note)*
	Broughte hire frendes out of sore	*sorrow*
	Thorw Jhesu Cristes grace.	
	Al the while that thei weore thare	
	The joye that was among hem yare	*prepared (provided)*
1235	No mon may telle the space.	
	Whon thei weore out of world iwent	*gone*
	Bifore God Omnipotent	
	Hem was diht a place.	*[For] them; prepared*
	Now Jhesu that is ful of miht	
1240	Graunt us alle in Hevene liht	
	To seo Thi swete face. AMEN.	

✿ EXPLANATORY NOTES

ABBREVIATIONS: **Ak**: National Library of Scotland Advocates MS 19.2.1 (the Auchinleck Manuscript); *CT*: Chaucer, *Canterbury Tales*, ed. Benson; **MED**: *Middle English Dictionary*; **OED**: *Oxford English Dictionary*; **Vernon**: Oxford, Bodleian Library 3938 (the Vernon Manuscript).

Title The title in Ak, "The King of Tars," is a marginal rubric over a small illumination. The picture presents the sultan praying to his idols, then praying with the princess at a (presumably) Christian altar. The Vernon manuscript prefaces the work with the descriptive title "Her bigineth of the Kyng of Trars / and of the Soudan of Dammas." See the appendix for other substantive readings from the Vernon.

2 *For Marie's love.* The poet here invokes the Virgin Mary, mother of Jesus. Devotion to the Virgin, while always part of popular Christianity, grew from the fifth century to flower in the high Middle Ages. Karen Saupe notes that in the twelfth century devotion of Mary assumed a preeminent role. Saupe observes that while Christ, who was human and divine, was also the judge "and therefore to be feared," Mary was a "virtuous virgin, queen of heaven, and loving human mother" and much more accessible as an intercessor for regular people (*Middle English Marian Lyrics*, p. 9). Her close relationship to Christ also gave her a special position that other saints did not have, further increasing her perceived power: "countless romances and secular poems begin or end with invocations to Mary. And of course she is the subject of hundreds of medieval poems, songs, carols, and prayers which survive today" (Saupe, *Middle English Marian Lyrics*, pp. 10–11). While the current poem is not a work devoted to the Virgin, its focus on a strong woman who gives birth to a miraculous child certainly responds to popular interest in Mary. Later in Ak are three works devoted to her: "The Nativity and Early Life of Mary" (folios 65v–69v), "The Assumption of the Blessed Virgin" (72r–78r), and "How Our Lady's Sauter was First Found" (259r–260v). For more on the contents of Ak, see the introduction, pp. 7, 17–18. For more on Mary and Marian devotion, see Miri Rubin, *Mother of God*.

6 *Dames.* Damascus was long a center of trade, religion, and learning, and, therefore, power. Its proximity to Jerusalem made it desirable to both Christians and Muslims. Unsuccessful Frankish attacks on Damascus in 1126 and 1129 were followed, in 1148, by an attempt to take the city that failed spectacularly and, as Christopher Tyerman posits, "destroyed the Second Crusade" (*God's War*, p. 335). Still, Damascene leaders considered the Franks to be the lesser threat, and often allied with them against their fellow Muslims until Saladin conquered the city in

1154. In the romance, it is a logical place to capture both the legendary East and still be convincing as a location close to a Christian kingdom.

7   *Tars.* A fictional Christian kingdom in the Orient. The word "tars" appears in *Sir Gawain and the Green Knight* (ed. Winny, lines 77, 571, and 858) and has sparked a fair amount of speculation regarding its location. Keith Harrison, translating *Sir Gawain and the Green Knight*, reads "Turkestan" in each instance, noting "The 'tars' of the original can be loosely interpreted to cover Turkestan, Turkey, and the biblical Tharsia — all places in the Orient such as could be associated with the silk trade" (*Sir Gawain and the Green Knight: A Verse Translation*, p. 92n5). Perryman identifies three possibilities for a real location: first, the poet may have meant "'Tartars', or 'the land of the Tartars', but there is a second possibility, that he intended *Tarsus*, the port in Armenia Minor" (p. 47); her third theory, anticipating Harrison's suggestion, is that "*Tars* was thought of by the romance writer as the mythical kingdom of Tharsia, located by Mandeville roughly in present-day Turkestan" (Perryman, p. 47). However, Perryman abandons this historicizing impulse at the end of her discussion of Tars as a real place, noting "the indefiniteness of the name *Tars* along with the lack of personal names for the chief protagonists would appear to be an aspect of the author's attempt to use names symbolically as part of the pattern of imagery expressing the poem's theme" (p. 49). The poet is clearly using the name as a fictional, Christian space in the Orient, much like the legends of Prester John, to heighten religious tension without the interference of specific political or historical readings.

11–16   *Non feirer woman . . . white swere.* The description of the princess is fairly standard and relies on formula to describe her beauty. Although, as Shores notes, "This catalogue is a conventional description of feminine beauty" (p. 200 n12–16A, V), the description of the princess emphasizes her appearance, and suggests that her beauty crosses cultural boundaries, appealing to all men. See the introduction for more on beauty and desire crossing cultural boundaries.

16   *lowe scholders.* Clearly a mark of beauty, "lowe" may indicate the shape of the princess's shoulders, suggesting they gently slope. It may also imply modesty or humility; Shores glosses *lowe* as "low, humble" (p. 281). I have glossed the adjective as "lovely" not to imply some form of love, but to emphasize the beauty of her body, particularly her shoulders in relation to her statuesque neck.

19–24   Although falling in love through hearsay is illogical according to modern conventions, it is commonplace in medieval romance. For an aristocratic audience used to arranged marriages, hearsay might have been enough to spur interest. Further, the princess is the most beautiful woman alive, and the sultan may be convinced that he deserves the best and so might overlook her faith in his objectification of women. A later close analogue can be found in Chaucer's Man of Law's Tale, where merchants spread the rumor of the beauty of the Roman princess, inflaming the desire of the sultan (*CT* II[B¹]171–89).

22   *his hert it brast ofive.* Shores dismisses any significance here, observing "the number 'five' is popular as a final word in metrical romance for purposes of rhyme. Its use

here, probably as a rhyme tag, has no profounder significance" (p. 200n22A, V), five being commonly affiliated with the body and the five senses. However, the sultan's heart breaking into five parts resonates with sensuality. The pentangle on Gawain's shield (*Sir Gawain and the Green Knight*, ed. Winny, lines 619–65) presumably protects him from such a bursting. There is further resonance with Jesus's five wounds (line 57) and Mary's five joys (line 785), both mentioned in this poem and also in the explication of Gawain's pentangle; see below (note 57) for more on the five wounds.

38   *wode*. This is the first of two instances of madness in the poem. Here, the king of Tars is nearly mad with grief; his daughter, whom he loves, is sacrificing herself to end a war that he is losing. His near madness is certainly reasonable, unlike the sultan's (see below, note 97–106). Regarding the frequent appearance of madness in romance, Mary Flowers Braswell notes "Madness, following the separation or estrangement from one's beloved, is a part of the courtly code (see, for example, Chaucer's Knight's Tale or 'Sir Orfeo')" (*Sir Perceval of Galles and Ywain and Gawain*, p. 196n1640). Although there is no romantic connection between the king and his daughter, his paternal love for her could certainly drive him nearly mad when he considers threats to her life and, in marrying a Saracen, her soul.

43   *Sarazin*. "Saracen" is generally used as a vague term for a heathen, pagan, or infidel in Middle English. Here, it refers specifically to Arab or Muslim opponents of Christianity, especially those fighting the (Christian) king of Tars.

45   *to drawe*. MED *drauen*, sense 2d, "to get, obtain." In response to the sultan of Damas's threat that he will win the princess by force if she is not sent to him (lines 31–33), the king of Tars suggests the sultan would have an easier time winning the devil than his daughter, unless she consents to the marriage and seals her own fate.

46–48 The meaning of these lines seems to be "Unless she will destroy herself through a marriage to him (the sultan), I do not know her thoughts."

57   *woundes five*. Christ's five wounds are those He suffered on the cross to His hands, feet, and side. They were considered especially symbolic of the Passion, and were celebrated as signs of Christ's special pains to buy salvation, as, for example, in *Sir Gawain and the Green Knight*, ed. Winny, lines 642–43.

72   *For thou hast him forsake*. An echo of line 55–57, where the king of Tars asks the princess if she will forsake Christ and she assures him she will not. The poet is engaging in wordplay here: the princess objects to the sultan, but will not abandon Christ.

80   *tit*. This word is difficult to gloss. Perryman, likely concurring with Shores, glosses this as "to fall as lot or portion" (Perryman, p. 107n80; Shores, p. 201n80A). They draw upon OED *tide*, sense 1. However, the word seems to be derived from *tiden*, "to happen, occur, come about; also, become (of sb.), happen (to sb.)" (*MED*, sense 1a). I have chosen to gloss it "he is not obliged" (*MED tiden*, sense 3) to account for the dative *him*. Thus, the king of Tars sends the sultan the

following message: "Think again, for concerning my daughter I have no obligation [to you]."

81   *For tresore no for rent.* The king has not, and will not, accept anything from the sultan, neither a one-time payment (*tresore*) nor ongoing income (*rent,* payment due to one's lord) from lands, for his daughter's hand. Though this refusal may be based on religious or moral grounds, it is fairly clear that the king deeply loves his daughter, and paternal affection should be considered as part of his position.

88   *prout in pres. MED* suggests "valiant in battle" (*proud,* sense 3b). An alternate reading might be "proud in [their] number," given the sultan's love of display.

92   *Of wicked wordes is nought scars.* An idiomatic understatement calling attention to the voluminous abuse the king of Tars laid upon the messengers in response to the sultan's proposal.

93   *Hethen hounde.* The poet does not specify all the abuse the king of Tars levels against the sultan, but, as Shores notes, this is "a popular romance insult for pagans" (p. 202n93A, V), and it is certainly in keeping with the situation. The hound imagery will reappear throughout the text, most notably during the princess's prophetic dream (lines 418–53).

97–108   Here is the second instance of uncontrollable anger, as the sultan goes completely berserk. His madness, unlike that of many others (see, e.g., Chrétien de Troyes's *Yvain* or its Middle English adaptation *Ywain and Gawain,* as well as Chaucer's *Knight's Tale*), is not provoked by love for another, but for himself; his is the madness of being denied a selfish claim. The sultan loses any semblance of control and civilization, as he rants and raves, tearing his clothing and beard.

98   *Also a wilde bore.* Boars are very fierce creatures, and boar-hunts are mentioned in all hunting manuals. According to the bestiary, the boar "signifies the fierceness of the rulers of this world" (*Bestiary,* trans. Barber, p. 87). The sultan's ferocity is about to be proven, both in the court and on the battlefield. But there are two further connections the poet likely wishes to invoke. First, the boar's spiritual significance, "the boar means the devil because of its fierceness and strength," could easily reflect upon the pagan sultan by virtue of his religion. Second, the boar "is said to be a creature of the woods because its thoughts are wild and unruly" (*Bestiary,* trans. Barber, p. 87). The sultan's reaction to the princess's refusal is entirely unreasonable, and he certainly acts like a boar in responding so wildly to the messengers.

102   *Seyn Mahoun.* An invocation of Mohammed, the founder of Islam. According to *MED,* "saint" can mean "pagan demigod or hero" (s.v. *seint(e,* sense 3a). Clearly the term here is meant to indicate status parallel to a Christian saint, not as a sign of reverence or respect. Later in the poem, Mahoun's status seems to change, as he is treated as an equal to the other pagan gods invoked by the Saracens. Perryman notes that Mahoun "was frequently treated as a heathen god or saint, especially in romances" (p. 107n102). It is likely that, in an attempt to create parallels to the Christian Trinity, Mahoun's status was becoming similar to

Christ's, a figure equally man and God, thus adding to the confusion of his status within this work.

107   *Serjaunt.* Shores glosses this as "sergeant," citing *OED sergeant* (p. 202n107A, V). However, the primary definition of "sergeaunt" in *MED* is "servingman, servant," and this meaning is certainly more in keeping with the figures one would meet in a court: servant, squire, clerk, knight, earl, and baron were all struck down by the raging sultan's actions which emphasize not only the sultan's madness, but also his indiscriminate violence.

125   *worthliche in wede.* This phrase has literal and figurative value here. Literally, it indicates that the princess is beautiful, important, or wealthy in clothes or in the world; as an idiom, it means honorable, noble, or respectable. Although *MED* (s.v. *wede*, n.2, sense f) also notes that it is "often used for alliteration or as a mere rhyme tag," it is more likely that the poet is playing with both the literal and figurative meanings, and not using the phrase simply to complete the line.

131–32   *Wrotherhele than was he been / Bot Y therto it bring.* The sultan here threatens the king of Tars, saying he has been brought to "wrother-heal," which *OED* defines as "misfortune, injury, calamity, or destruction," or perhaps he is threatened "with evil intention." The sultan has taken it upon himself to bring this evil fortune to the king of Tars for rejecting his request to marry the princess. Shores reads the referent for "it" in line 132 as "the marriage mentioned in 126A," but the text reads more smoothly if "it" refers to the king of Tars's misfortune or the sultan's evil response (p. 203n131 f.A, 125 f.V).

141   *hauberk of meile.* A coat of mail, or hauberk, was a set of interlocked rings that stretched from the head or shoulders to the mid-leg. It was the primary armor before the advent of plate armor. See David Nicolle, *Medieval Warfare*, pp. 195–96.

145   *unride.* *MED* defines "unride" as "numerous, monstrous" (*unride*, adj., sense 2a). While the poet likely intends both connotations, the context seems to call for a large company, rather than a wild one.

153   *maiden hende.* "Hende" means courteous or pleasant; the poet is being complimentary to the princess, suggesting her worth is not only in her appearance (see lines 10–18), but also in her personality and high intelligence.

155   *Seynt Eline.* Saint Helen (c. 250–330) was the mother of the Roman emperor Constantine (r. 306–77). She converted late in life (c. 312), though her legend says she had lived a Christian life prior to conversion. She discovered the True Cross while on pilgrimage, and her son nurtured Christianity, ultimately accepting baptism on his deathbed. Interest in Helen has a fairly long history in England, including Cynewulf's Old English poem *Elene* and a connection to English bloodlines in Geoffrey of Monmouth, where she is the daughter of King Coel (*History of the Kings of Britain*, p. 132). For the legend of Helen's discovery of the True Cross, see Jacobus de Voragine, *Golden Legend*, pp. 269–76.

    the thridde in May. May 3 is actually the Feast of the Invention ("finding") of the Cross by St. Helen, in whose honor the saint's day is established; see John McCall, "Chaucer's May 3," pp. 201–05, and Russell A. Peck, "Numerology and Chaucer's

Troilus and Criseyde," pp. 28–29. In the church calendar, Helen's feast day is August 18. The third of May appears three times in Chaucer's works, once in *Troilus and Criseyde* and twice in the *Canterbury Tales.* Book 2 of *Troilus and Criseyde* opens on May 3, when Pandarus feels the pain of love and sleeps poorly before he begins to woo Criseyde for Troilus. In the Knight's Tale (*CT* I(A)1462–63), this is the date of Palamon's escape from prison. Finally, in The Nun's Priest's Tale (*CT* VII[B²]3187–90), Chauntecleer's misfortunes begin when he encounters the fox on May 3. For the King of Tars, May 3 is an unlucky day on which he begins a losing war. See also George R. Adams and Bernard S. Levy, "Good and Bad Fridays and May 3 in Chaucer," pp. 245–48. Perryman suggests that the conflation of the two feasts (the Invention and Helen's) may account for the "surprising scarcity of entries for this saint in English church calendars . . . considering her great popularity" (p. 108n155). The Vernon's reading, "Withthinne the thridde day of May," avoids the error.

158   *bright armour and brod baner.* The sultan is clearly a sight to see here. His armor suggests several possibilities. Its brightness could be a sign of his wealth, in that his armor is either new or properly cleaned; it may also be a sign that he is not battle-weary, and possibly not experienced. His broad banner further adds to his visibility, as is appropriate for the leader of a medieval force; soldiers could see their leader and draw upon his guidance and presence. Further, its breadth is a sign of power in itself; the sultan carries no small pennant, as so many knights in the Bayeux Tapestry do, but a broad banner, a large symbol of his presence and importance.

172   *That men might sen alle the fen.* The reading in Ak is obviously a corruption since "that men might sen alle the fen" makes little sense, unlike the Vernon reading — "falde hem doun in þe fen [mud/dirt]." Perhaps "fen" should be read as a metaphor in response to line 170 and anticipating line 174, hence my gloss "bloody mess."

177   *Mani a frely rode.* Both Perryman and Shores emend Ak's "frely rode" to "frely fode." Shores glosses this as "noble or worthy man" (p. 203n177A, 171V). Perryman is silent in her notes, but identifies "fode" as "young warrior" [*sic*] in her glossary (p. 115). I have retained Ak's "rode" as the poet's intention and glossed accordingly, in keeping with the context of a large battle. See *MED rode,* n.3, senses 1a and c.

205–07   The king of Tars sees the newly-invogorated sultan of Damascus leap into the battle and slay many of his knights, and he flees to the safety of his city rather than remaining on the battlefield.

220   *palle.* Tars's daughter, having refused to wed the sultan, now is filled with remorse over the slaughter of both Christians and Muslims. *Palle* is a fine cloth (See Vernon, line 358 "in cloth or riche purpel palle," appendix p. 87), associated with royalty but also with mourning, as in the funeral pall over the coffin, or with religious connotations as in purity robes or an altar cloth. Here the poet is perhaps combining two senses of the term as the daughter comes both as the princess but

also as one in mourning over the waste of life that she has perpetrated by her earlier decision. See Castleberry, "Devils in the Bridal Chamber."

223–24 *lete me be the soudan's wiif / And rere na more cuntek no striif.* Winstead observes, "*The King of Tars* applauds a 'saint' who stops at nothing to protect her family, obey her husband, and safeguard her people" ("Saints, Wives, and Other 'Hooly Thynges,'" p. 145). She will be a martyr herself before letting the slaughter continue. But the uniqueness of her "martyrdom" sets her apart from the usual female Christian saints, who would die before letting their bodies be defiled.

229–31 *Y wil serve . . . And leve on God almight.* The princess tells her father of her plan to deceive the sultan. She will continue to believe in Christianity, though she will properly serve the sultan as his wife. Such heroines as the princess of Tars, Constance, and Emaré "rely on and have undaunting faith in God. The heroines are not only examples to other Christians, but they also win souls for God. The author makes stalwart heroes out of passive women. They do not only have the fighting-power of classical heroes, but they are converters, soul winners and savers. Through the 'activeness' of their faith these heroines are favored by God, are spiritual role models and deal with adversity with bravado" (Cordery, "Medieval Interpretation of Risk," p. 184).

230 *bothe loude and stille.* That is, at all times. To end the war, the princess wishes to accede to the sultan's demands and to be a dutiful wife, but she also plans to retain her faith as part of her true devotion and to console her father, perhaps as foreshadowing.

244 *thou wilt save thi moder and me.* The king recognizes that his the daughter's sacrifice will save them all.

260 *For now er here bot we thre.* The king's meaning is ambiguous. Perhaps they are the last three who can save the Christians, who are being slaughtered by the sultan's overwhelming force.

261 *kende.* There is no easy gloss for this word, which is like the Latin term *gens.* It indicates a group and can variously mean "kind," "species," or, most commonly, "nature" in the sense of "essential characteristics." But its use here, "Cristen kende," suggests a group that is not genetic but spiritual, and I have glossed accordingly. See *MED kinde,* n., especially sense 10a.

265–76 The princess shows a great deal of personal character and initiative here, anticipating some of Chaucer's women, such as patient Griselda, who suffers her husband's capricious test (The Clerk's Tale); Saint Cecilia, who converts her husband (The Second Nun's Tale); and especially Constance, who was married to the sultan of Syria on condition of his conversion to Christianity (The Man of Law's Tale). See the introduction, p. 17, for more on Chaucer's potential connection to Ak.

271 *thrawe.* Shores glosses this as "anguish," tentatively deriving it from Old English "þrawu," meaning threat, oppression, or calamity (p. 309). I have instead glossed it as Middle English "throu," meaning a space of time; thus, lines 271–72 read "Therefore I will suffer Christians to be slain for me no longer." *MED throu,*

n.1, sense 1a cites three other instances of this use from Ak: *Arthur and Merlin*, lines 6713 and 9681, and *Guy of Warwick (2)*, p. 146 (line 824 in *Stanzaic Guy of Warwick*, ed. Wiggins).

274 *with wordes stille*. Though women are usually portrayed as submissive to their parents and husbands, that does not mean they are voiceless or mindlessly malleable. Here, the daughter speaks with calm determination to both father and mother. The exemplary spiritual behavior of women like the princess "lifts these women above the submissiveness of their worldly existence: they become submissive to a higher authority — to God. The heroines show attributes the audience should wish to emulate. They strike an alliance of faith with God, Jesus, Mary and the saints. This gives them the courage to challenge risk and the strength to fight adversity" (Cordery, "Medieval Interpretation of Risk," p. 184).

276 *With resoun right and even*. The princess has control over her mind, and uses logic to persuade her parents that her plan is good. Though it is not generally acceptable for a Christian to wed a Saracen, it is proper for a princess to protect her people. The description of the princess's mind as "even" should evoke a sense of impartiality and deliberation, in direct opposition to the rash, emotional reactions of the sultan.

290 *pers*. As the next line makes clear, his "peers" are the dukes, princes, and kings of his land. The term also evokes the twelve peers of Charlemagne romances, the greatest warriors of Charlemagne's kingdom. Two of the *douseperes*, Roland and Otuel, are featured in separate romances also present in Ak: "Roland and Vernagu" (fol. 262v stub–267v) and "Otuel, a Knight" (fol. 268r–277v). Like the invocation of Mary (see note 2, above), medieval readers could be expected to be familiar with the characters through the store of common knowledge, as well as by reading these pieces.

302 *Arliche and late, loude and stille*. These adverbial phrases essentially mean "at all times," amplifying the princess's submission of line 230. The sultan of Damascus makes peace with the king of Tars, and respects his position as his father-in-law, promising to help the king of Tars at any time.

308 *Bothen hem was wele and wo*. Unlike other pairs of contradictory words, as in lines 230 and 302, the contradiction here indicates conflict, rather than being "an empty phrase meaning 'all circumstances'" (Perryman, p. 109n308). The king and queen are simultaneously glad that the war has ended and sad that their Christian daughter is marrying the pagan sultan to bring about that peace.

309 *In rime also we rede*. Here, as well as in other places throughout the text, the tension between written and oral presentation of the text is expressed. Although it is possible to read these lines as stock phrases, there is a shift through the text from primarily reading the text to hearing it.

323 *Of gret pité now may ye here*. This is one of the places where the narrator interrupts the poem to control the audience's response, and suggests an oral presentation as much as a written one.

338–39   *the soudan . . . so noble a knight.* The queen's position is difficult to construe here. She means no disrespect to the sultan in calling him a knight; that is, it is no demotion, but simply a polite way to refer to the sultan's positive, "chivalric" qualities, those associated with knighthood in the romances. It may be that she also recognizes the nobility of the sultan; however, it is unclear if this is because she is resigned to her daughter's marriage and wants to make the best of it, or because he is of Saracen nobility. Her next statement, in lines 344–48, is similarly cryptic, as her observation that her daughter is "noght to him to gode" (not too good for him) disparages her daughter. Perryman explains the statements by noting that the queen is submissive to the conqueror, "as is indicated by her *milde chere*" in line 343 (p. 109n344–8).

349–57   This stanza only has nine lines, rather than the standard twelve. Perryman adds three lines, based on Vernon, within brackets between lines 354 and 355: "Thai seye it might non other go; / Bitaughten hir god for evermo / And kist her douhter thare." Ak omits this touching scene where the king and queen of Tars see their daughter off, potentially for the last time.

353   *Her sorwe couthe thai no man kithe.* "Kithe," here glossed as "reveal," could also mean "describe"; that is, their sorrow was boundless, a reading supported by their initial resistance to allowing their daughter to wed the sultan. However, it is more likely that at this point, they must not reveal their unhappiness in order to save their kingdom and religion. The danger of their sorrow is reinforced by lines 356–57, which suggests they can only release their grief in private. This kind of disingenuous action is later echoed by the princess, who professes one faith in public (i.e., Islam) and practices another in private (i.e., Christianity).

368   *Hem chaunged bothe hide and hewe.* Unlike the sultan's metamorphosis (lines 922–24), the transformation of the king and queen of Tars is due to sadness, as they lose their daughter through her self-sacrifice.

371   *telle we of that maiden ying.* In comparing romances with saints' lives, Winstead observes, "we find that romance writers were in fact combining the familiar stories about virtuous women, sexual persecution, and miraculous deliverance with a new kind of protagonist, a revised set of priorities, and a different system of values. Romances consistently upheld the figures of authority that virgin martyrs had scoffed at — husbands, fathers, judges, and rulers; they extolled the conjugal and filial duites that virgin martyrs had spurned; and they transformed the commanding protagonists of hagiography into [seemingly] passive objects of man's hatred or desire" ("Saints, Wives, and Other 'Hooly Thynges,'" p. 141; the addition is mine). The princess will, in fact, be exceedingly strong in her hidden behavior and will bridge the presentation of women in the two distinct genres.

380–81   *sche was cladde / As hethen wiman ware.* The princess was earlier dressed in fine clothing ("palle," line 218). Here, the clothing itself distinguishes the two cultures; the princess, to become a "heathen," must first look the part by wearing the right clothes. A similar re-dressing occurs in Chaucer's Clerk's Tale, where Griselda is stripped and clothed anew when she enters Walter's household as his wife (*CT* IV[E]372–78), though her change is one of status, from poverty to riches, rather than a betrayal of culture.

389   *bright on ble*. This is a fairly standard phrase for "beautiful." The poet also calls attention to a racial distinction here, since the (Christian) princess is white, and the (Saracen) court is black. See also the sultan's conversion, lines 922–24 and note, below.

391–93 The princess's sorrow parallels that of her parents (lines 358–69). However, unlike the king and queen, who are surrounded by supportive people, the princess is alone, and no one might prevent or ease her sadness.

400–10 Islam is presented as a mirror of Christianity here; the sultan will not wed the princess without her conversion. Clearly, he too recognizes the gulf between their religions and does not allow sexual desire to bridge it. Marriage between a Christian princess and a Saracen king is a common first stage of the Constance group, perhaps best known through Chaucer's Man of Law's Tale and Gower's Tale of Constance (*Confessio Amantis*, ed. Peck, 2.587–1612). The different religions of the sultan and princess are a barrier, and while Gower's sultan of Persia and Chaucer's sultan of Syria both offer to convert to entice Constance to wed them, Chaucer's Man of Law specifically notes the difficulty they face: "They trowe that no 'Cristen prince woulde fayn / Wedden his child under oure lawe'" (*CT* II[B²]222–23). Like a Christian man (line 406), the sultan of Damas is loath to wed someone who does not share his faith, but he does not offer to convert; unlike Gower and Chaucer, this poet wishes to play out a true conversion rather than allow a Saracen to convert for lustful reasons. There are few marriages in medieval literature that cross religious lines; perhaps the most successful is between the Christian knight Gahmuret and Muslim queen Belacane in Wolfram von Eschenbach's German poem *Parzival*. The offspring of that marriage, Feirfiz, ultimately accepts Christianity as the true law and converts, as will the sultan. Contrast the more romantic religous miscegenation in *Floris and Blanchefleur*, where religious convictions, whether Christian or Muslim, are swiftly overwhelmed by true love.

418–53 Prophetic dream visions, as here, are fairly common in medieval literature, though this one is poignantly frightening to the princess. But it is also hopeful. It reassures her that her trials will lead, through her faith, to a good ending. This trope is popular in hagiography, where the saint is often martyred, but it is also popular in romance; for example, Yvain/Ywain has to reinvent himself to regain his true love, and Gowther has to abandon his very identity before he has atoned for his sins and is rewarded with high status and, ultimately, sainthood. As mentioned above, the hound imagery is a clear denigration of the Saracens, a metaphor that is carried throughout the text but nowhere else made so explicitly fearsome.

431   *gleive*. *MED* defines "gleive" as "a weapon with a long shaft ending in a point or an attached blade; lance, spear." This sort of glaive was also used by footsoldiers. While the earliest cited reference, *Debate of the Body and Soul* (c. 1300), includes "swords" (*Desputisoun*, ed. Linow, p. 98) as a variant in Digby MS 102, in *Havelok*

the Dane and *Stanzaic Guy of Warwick*, both present in Ak, the weapon appears to be a spear or lance: "Axes and gisarmes scharp ygrounde / And glaives forto give with wounde" (*Stanzaic Guy of Warwick*, ed. Wiggins, lines 3088–89; see also that poem's lines 2175 and 3005, and *Havelok the Dane*, lines 1748 and 1770).

446–48   Christ here appears in the guise of a knight. This widespread image appears in the *Gesta Romanorum*; Langland's *Piers Plowman*, passus 18; and Henryson's "The Bludy Serk," among other places. See Rosemary Woolf's article "Theme of Christ the Lover-Knight" for more examples of "one of the commonest allegories in medieval preaching books and manuals of instruction" (p. 1).

448   *white clothes*. This term refers to a white surcoat worn over armor. The Vernon variant *whit armuyre*, indicating shining armor, "probably reflects the change during the fourteenth century from chain mail to full plate armour of polished steel" (Perryman, p. 109n451).

450   *No tharf thee nothing*. An instance of amplification of the negative, not a double negative.

451   *Ternagaunt*. One of the most common names for the Saracen trinity's version of the Father. The *OED* identifies "Ternagant" or "Termagant" as "an imaginary deity held in mediæval Christendom to be worshipped by Muslims" (s.v. *termagant*). The term is used repeatedly in *Bevis of Hampton* (see, e.g., lines 659, 1380, and 1510), and appears in the *Tale of Ralph the Collier* (line 850) and Henryson's "The Annunciation" (line 68) as a name for the devil.

454–56   The princess awakens from her nightmare shaking from both fear and love. She fears the vision she was shown, but loves the reassurance the Christ-knight brings her that her story will have a happy conclusion.

460–62   The syntax here is compressed. "Schuld" has no clear subject, which is implied. The passage indicates the princess hopes that, just as her dream promised (lines 418–53), her current situation will end well.

465   *temple*. While the word was used to describe any place of worship, *MED* emphasizes its pagan connotations: "A building dedicated to the worship of a pagan god or gods or which housed an idol" (*temple*, sense 1).

467–77   The sultan attempts to convert the princess through the threat of violence. Because of his own zealous faith, he is convinced he is correct, and he insults the "fals lay" of Christianity (line 469), echoing the rhetoric of Christian proselytization. But he is unable to convert the princess because she too has strong faith, and her dream bolsters her belief in the true religion, Christianity.

474   *Jovin and Plotoun*. Two of the heathen gods, Jovin and Plotoun are linguistically based on the Roman gods Jove (or Jupiter, god of the sky and king of the gods) and Pluto (god of the underworld), but are here simply included as names of the false idols to which the Saracens pray and are probably not intended to carry further significance, though there certainly are similarities between Pluto's abduction of Persephone and the sultan's taking of the princess. Perhaps their

top to bottom pairing implies inclusion of all the false gods in between, who subsequently are repeatedly enumerated.

478–89   Although she attends and participates in the pagan ceremonies, the princess does not abandon Christianity but only appears to convert. The fact that her conversion is not true is reflected in the lack of a physical change to reflect the spiritual change, unlike the later metamorphoses of the sultan and their child. See below, notes 769–77 on the child's baptism and 922–24 on the sultan's conversion. The princess's "mild chere" (line 478) is also worth noting because it echoes her mother's demeanor in line 343, where the queen resignedly offers her daughter to the sultan. Both women are in difficult positions, and hope for a more hallowed outcome. See also note 371 above.

480–89   The princess's conversion here is socially correct. She asks that her husband teach her the names, manners, and rituals of her new home. However, she subtly indicates her actual belief in lines 485–86, where she still acknowledges Christ as the maker of mankind. She also says to herself that she is serving her husband the sultan, not the pagan gods he invokes in lines 474–75.

491–500   *Mahoun . . . Jubiter.* The pagan gods are named as the princess kisses each of the idols. Mahoun and Ternagant have been mentioned above (see notes 102 and 451). Jovin and Jubiter are both names for Jove or Jupiter, which, like Apolin (Apollo), is derived from Greco-Roman myth. Astirot has been identified with the Sidonian goddess "Astarthe" of 1 Kings 11:5 and 33 (Shores p. 206n497A; Perryman p. 110n500). Gower, *Confessio Amantis*, picks up on Solomon's worship of Astrathen, "Sche of Sidoyne" (ed. Peck, 7.4499–4502), to define Solomon's lechery, given his affiliation with sexuality and child bearing, which has some bearing on the sultan's begetting capacity. In this regard, however, the sultan is notably unlecherous. Arthur Cotterell describes Astarthe as an aggressive warrior goddess of Mesopotamian myth (*Dictionary of World Mythology*, p. 20), and this is in keeping with the characterization of the Saracens in this poem. The final god in this heathen pantheon, Plotoun (Pluto, line 474), is omitted from this list, likely because of meter.

492   *biknawe.* The sultan thanks Mahoun for the princess's conversion to Islam, ignorant of her duplicity. The word might also be glossed as "wise." This reading would highlight the ambiguity of the princess's false conversion, as she maintains the true faith, showing proper wisdom. The line could also be read as "that she so acknowledged [Islam]." See *MED biknouen*, sense 3, which means to "acknowledge . . . (a doctrine)."

497   As Perryman observes (p. 110n500), Jove and Jupiter (line 500) are treated as separate pagan gods, despite being the same figure in Roman mythology.

498   *For drede of wordes awe.* The phrase "wordes awe" has a multitude of meanings. Perryman explores the possibilities, concluding this line "could mean 'on account of the fear of scorn' or 'for fear of the threatening of men'. Even though 'world' does not usually lack an *l* in Ak, the latter is probably the correct sense, a reading supported by the Vernon's and the Simeon's unambiguous *worldes*

awe" (p. 110n501). It is clearly a reference to the sultan's threat in lines 472–73 ("And certes, bot thou wilt [convert] anon, / Thi fader Y schal with wer slon").

502–13   The princess here begins her deceit of her husband, the sultan, for religious reasons. Such a decision is at odds with the hagiographical themes in the tale, however. As Winstead observes, "Though the writer of *The King of Tars* emphasizes that his heroine only pretends to embrace paganism (507–16), in traditional saints' lives such equivocation was never an option. The conclusion to *The King of Tars*, in fact, suggests that setting aside religious scruples can actually work to the greater glory of God, for the protagonist's willingness to obey her husband, even to the point of 'conversion,' is richly rewarded: a specular miracle causes the sultan to repudiate his idols, and, aided by the King of Tars, the newly converted monarch compels his entire empire to adopt Christianity. In effect, the tale demonstrates that women can bring about momentous feats simply by submitting to their husbands, serving their parents, and trusting God" ("Saints, Wives, and Other 'Hooly Thynges,'" p. 146).

506   *minstral*. Although the context makes it clear that the minstrel here is an entertainer (*MED*, sense 1), it is not clear why the minstrel would be responsible for changing the princess's beliefs. Perhaps the poet is overestimating the entertainer's ability to make the truth plain through literature, though it is more likely that the poet is indicating the princess's fixation on Christianity, not forgetting Christ (line 504) even when potentially distracted by a variety of entertainments. She certainly did not forget her faith when participating in the presumably solemn Saracen rites, and this may be an attempt to juxtapose religious and secular events.

   crouthe. The crwth is a fairly square Welsh stringed instrument, reminiscent of a lyre, played with a bow; Anthony Baines notes that it may have been plucked initially (*Oxford Companion to Musical Instruments*, p. 86). Henry Holland Carter identifies it "with light musical entertainment," citing *The King of Tars*, "Sir Tristrem," and "Lybeaus Desconus," among others (*Dictionary of Middle English Musical Terms*, p. 105).

514–19   Celebratory tournaments are a common romance device; compare *Perceval of Gales*, Malory's "Tale of Sir Gareth," and *The Tournament of Tottenham*, where tournaments are staged for the bride's sake (line 525). Dubbing new knights is a common feature of tournaments.

520   *trumpes*. Although the more common meaning is "a type of wind instrument," the word was transferred to the player, or "trumpeter" in the Ak "Beves of Hamptoun" (line 3793; Perryman, p. 111n523). Both "trump" and "trumpeter" fit the context here.

529–37   Unlike the highly elaborate events that appear in later romances, the tournament here seems to be a violent melee intended to help train knights for battle. It was this early form that led the church to condemn tournaments in 1179. Shores too points out that the princess observes the tournament from the castle, thus emphasizing her "isolation from the Christian world" (p. 207n526–528A, 499–501V), though that has been the place for the observation of such contests since the beginning of literary history. See the *Iliad*, Book 3. In this instance, both the sultan and his queen observe from the rampart as if to judge the melee in their honor.

548   *In the maner of his lay.* The poet is again drawing parallels and distinctions between Saracens and Christians. Following the tournament, the sultan and princess are wed in a lawful ceremony, as is appropriate for either culture; however, the ceremony itself is a Saracen one, not a Christian wedding. It is another reminder that the princess is in a foreign land and further isolated from what she knows.

554   *Of harp and fithel and of gest.* Harps and fiddles were fairly common instruments resembling their modern counterparts. "Gest" has been emended from Ak "grest." Krause read the three nouns as parallel in this construction, and suggested a lost instrument to explain the word "grest" ("Kleine publicationen," p. 46n554). Bliss questioned this reading, suggesting instead emendation to "wrest," meaning "plectrum" or "tuning-key" ("Notes on 'The King of Tars,'" p. 461). Shores supports Bliss's suggestion, noting his reading "seems best because his word . . . is a musical term in keeping with the other nouns in the line" (pp. 207–08n554A). Perryman emends to "gest," supposing that the story would be "told or possibly chanted to musical accompaniment" (Perryman, p. 111n557). While I agree with Perryman's emendation, I think the repetition of the preposition *of* suggests a parallel entertainment, a tale told with or without musical accompaniment; that is, the minstrels entertained the court with music and recitations. The melody (line 553) could be understood simply as the meter and cadence of the poetry.

565   *When it was geten, sche chaunged ble.* Each of the major characters in the poem undergoes some transformation, and the princess now changes with pregnancy. Unlike the sultan and their child, who undergo miraculous physical changes, the princess undergoes a reasonable, natural change. This is much more in keeping with her Christian parents, who changed "hide and huwe" (line 368) out of sorrow. The princess's change may be simple biology (*MED ble*, sense 3a, "appearance"), though it may indicate a change in the princess's expression as she realizes she is pregnant (*MED ble*, sense 2b, "facial expression; countenance"). All we are told is that the princess prayed for deliverance from shame (line 570).

572   *deliverd o bende.* "Bende" has a number of meanings, primarily relating to imprisonment, and there are three deliveries here, all contingent on the birth. *MED* initially lists the physical bindings for *bende*: "fetter," "shackle," "chain"; "a cord for tying or fastening." Figurative meanings include "a legal or moral commitment." The second definition primarily describes captivity, including "imprisonment of the soul within the body," and mentions the phrase "bringen (out) of ~" as release from "confinement in childbearing." Here, the princess is delivered of child and released from the limited mobility of her pregnancy. In addition, her delivery from Islam and her false conversion begins here, as the story will show.

574–82   The child is absolutely formless, having no limbs or face. It is also born without life. Scholars have commented on the child's resemblance to bear cubs; here is an excerpt from an early eleventh-century Latin bestiary:

> The bear gets its Latin name 'ursus' because it shapes its cubs with its mouth, from the Latin word 'orsus'. For they are said to give birth to shapeless lumps of flesh, which the mother licks into shape. The bear's tongue forms the young which it brings forth." (*Bestiary*, trans. Barber, p. 58)

The legend of the bear's formless birth appears in Aristotle, Ovid, Isidore, and others; see Lillian Herlands Hornstein, "Folklore Theme," p. 83n14, for an overview. Lions are likewise said to give birth to dead offspring, who are animated after three days by the breath of their father (*Bestiary*, trans. Barber, pp. 24–25); this text does not draw that parallel, as the child's father (the sultan) is utterly incapable of breathing life into the child, and it is animated after an unspecified amount of time, though it is probably a matter of hours rather than days.

587–91   *Ogain mi godes thou art forsworn . . . Alle thurth thi fals bileve.* The sultan correctly reads the monstrous birth as a sign of the religious gulf between himself and the princess. Although he is correct in reading the cause of the sign, the princess will prove to him that his premise is wrong: it is not the gods to which he prays that have created the lump-child, but her God that has arranged for these circumstances.

600–18   In response to the sultan's rage at the lump-child, the princess calmly proposes a test of faith. If the sultan can prove his gods' power by making the flesh have form and life, she will properly and truly convert. But if he fails, she will prove Christianity true by giving the flesh form, and he will have to convert. Her faith and the dream, along with the conventions within which the tale is working and the audience's expectations, converge to give the princess courage and conviction that the sultan will fail.

602   *For thi bileve it farth so.* The princess claims it is not her fault the child is unformed, but the sultan's; since the princess has accepted the truth of Christianity, it is the sultan's heathen faith that has created the misshapen child. Although this specific misshapen birth was not foreseen, it certainly speaks to fears of miscegenation raised earlier in the poem and current in medieval thought. See the introduction, pp. 13–16, and note 400–10, above.

611   *Make it fourmed after a man.* This phrasing echoes the creation story of Genesis, where the Lord forms Adam in His own image (1:26–27). The ability to create or bestow form is very important to this poem, as the re-forming of the lump-child's body and sultan's spirit are at the core of this poem. The episode also echoes the Christian idea that humans need to be born again, that is, spiritually re-born through baptism. The image of Christ as creator is repeated in lines 512–13, 603, 674, and 689.

614–16   *Y schal leve thee better than / That thai ar ful of might. / And bot thai it to live bring.* The princess will not believe in the power of the heathen gods unless they bring life to the lump-child, as Christ did with Lazarus (John 11:1–44) or Himself, in the resurrection. This is a change from the implications of her earlier, deceitful actions, wherein she appeared to convert, but "Jhesu forgat sche nought" (line 504). The princess, much like the Jews of John 11:45, will believe in the power and truth of another religion only through a display of great power, bringing life to the lifeless.

624   *While men might go five mile.* The sultan makes an honest effort, praying for the time it would take a man to walk five miles, about an hour and a half. He is no dilettante, simply carrying on the religious traditions, but he truly believes in his gods and their power to affect the lump-child. This depth of character is in contrast to Queen Bramimonde and the pagans in *The Song of Roland* who, after losing to Charlemagne's army, rage against their idols, including Apollo and Termagaunt. See *The Song of Roland*, trans. Brault, lines 2578–91, 2694–97, and especially 2711–18.

627   *In you was never no gile.* In anti-Muslim propaganda, Mohammed was said to be a convincing deceiver. One story claims "he trained a dove to pick seeds of corn from his ear so as to persuade the people that he was receiving communications from the Holy Ghost" (Saunders, *History of Medieval Islam*, p. 35). Such tales of deceit would have been popular with Christians, who believed in the fundamental falsity of Islam. Clearly, the sultan is faithful, and believes — but Christian audiences might recall this or a similar tale, and be amused by the claim of honesty.

629   *Astirot.* The invocation of Astarte (Ishtar/Venus) is especially apt here, as she is a goddess of fertility, sexuality, and birthing. See note to lines 491–500 above.

630   *perile.* Although the sultan is in no physical danger from the lump of flesh he placed on the altar, he is right to pray to his gods to save him from the spiritual and social danger the lump-child represents. The *MED* defines *peril* as "a perilous situation, condition, object, or place" (sense 1b), which certainly describes the sultan's position: he has sired a monstrous child, a sign of celestial disapproval. Knowledge of the lump-child could threaten the sultan's position. But it is perhaps another sense that best fits the tone of the poem: "spiritual peril, danger to the soul from sin" (*MED*, sense 2); the sin here is his marriage to an unbeliever.

637–57   The sultan, incensed at the idols' inability to show any power, rages against them, throwing them down in a spectacular display reminiscent of Moses destroying the golden calf (Genesis 32:19–20) and Jesus in the temple casting out the moneylenders (Matthew 21:12, Mark 11:15, and John 2:13–14). Their arms and heads broken off, the pagan gods now become lumps, a further commentary on the sultan's principle talent at this phase of his life. The characteristic nature of Saracens toward rash, violent action is often featured in medieval literature; see, e.g., Marsila in *The Song of Roland*, Laban in "The Sultan of Babylon," and the sultan's mother in Chaucer's Man of Law's Tale.

663–68   *Lo, have it here. . . help me nought.* One must admire the honesty and integrity of the sultan. Though he flies into a rage when provoked by the idols' inaction, he does not fool himself with false pretenses but faces the truth head on. This is an important step in his conversion.

672   *Leve sir.* "Beloved sir" or "Dear sir," an expression of her courtesy, seems the most appropriate gloss here (compare line 679), but the phrase might also be "Leve, sir," that is, "With your permission." Though the *MED* does not cite the phrase as an idiom of address, either reading emphasizes the wife's obedience and high respect for her husband and the moment that is about to ensue, not only giving life to her child but providing her with a true husband. A third resonance, as well, is affirmed in line 680, where "leve" means "believe." In line 672, the sultan will begin to believe when he hears and witnesses her speech as she sets out to "teach" him ("ichil you teche," line 675).

672–73 *here mi speche. / The best rede that Y can.* Like Custance, Dame Prudence, or Lady Philosophy, the sultaness modestly assumes the role of counsellor, which is appropriate to her role as Sapientia, the wise woman.

676   *Nou thou hast proved god thine.* "Proved" can mean both "tested" or "proven." Both seem to be suitable glosses here, though "proven" seems more appropriate, as the sultan has proven his gods' inability to give the child form, and therefore their falsity.

685   *Now, dame, ichil do bi thi lore.* The "dame's" patient instruction of her husband epitomizes the behavior of a virtuous wife. Winstead makes the point that "One possible attraction is that legends of virtuous wives, like romances of pious knights, provided paradigms of holiness that were more congenial to lay life than those in contemporary saints' lives. Virgin martyr legends upheld traditional clerical values, such as celibacy and contempt for the world. Hagiographers presented their heroines as invulnerable champions of the faith and efficacious intercessors, whose actions were surely intended to be admired rather than imitated. With their contempt for secular life and their miraculous imperviousness to pain, the protagonists of Middle English hagiography had little in common with ordinary people. Pious romances, by contrast, offered heroines whose desires and cares lay readers could readily understand. These romances asserted the worth of family and society, and they assured readers that it was not necessary to forswear wealth and worldly happiness in the pursuit of heaven. Echoing a theme we encounter frequently in late medieval didactic literature, they also affirmed that a good woman does not forfeit her 'hoolynesse' through marriage and sexual activity. In effect, pious romances conveyed the comforting message that a prosperous wife could be as worthy of praise as a virgin martyr" ("Saints, Wives, and Other 'Hooly Thynges,'" pp. 151–52).

693   *As icham gentil knight.* The sultan swears by his knighthood, not by his crown. This may be a means to identify him with the audience but is more likely a reference to the expectation in romance that knighthood is a sign of worthiness. That is, knights are expected to be good (i.e., chivalrous), whereas kings can be ruthless. See also note 338–39, where the queen of Tars refers to the sultan's knighthood.

714   *maumettes*. This is the first time the pagan gods are described as idols. The word
        is derived (through Old French) from Mohammed, "resulting from the common
        medieval Christian belief that the prophet Muhammad was worshipped as a
        god" (*OED*). The fact that the princess calls them such may be a sign that she is
        gathering her will and is preparing to attack the sultan's faith directly.

730   *bi Seyn Jon*. Cleophas's invocation of Saint John is likely idiomatic. Although there
        is no shortage of saints named John for him to call upon, other appearances of
        the saint in the text suggest that Cleophas calls upon John the Baptist. He was
        "immensely popular" in medieval England (Farmer, *Oxford Dictionary of Saints*,
        p. 264), and his invocation here is particularly appropriate, given the conversion
        narrative that begins in earnest at this point. See also lines 767–68 and note.

738   *And tow wilt held thee stille*. The princess's advice to be "stille" works on three
        levels. First, and most directly, the princess tells the priest to "be quiet." Further,
        she implicitly advises the priest to "be patient" and listen to her. Finally, she asks
        the priest to "be humble," trusting in her plan, which relies on restraint,
        patience, and humility to be successful — three things the sultan has not been,
        but that are important for Christians. She then presents the secret plan to the
        priest, who will help convert the sultan and, ultimately, the entirety of Damas.

739–40 *For thurth thine help in this stounde, / We schul make Cristen men of houndes*. The
        hound imagery again appears, here suggesting the subhuman status of non-
        Christians. These lines also suggest the transformative power of baptism, as it
        can change hounds into men, anticipating the miraculous changes of the lump-
        child (lines 769–77) and sultan (lines 922–24).

742   *the soudan's wiif*. This is the fourth term used for the princess, and its significance
        is worth consideration. While she is in Tars, she is referred to as a maiden or
        daughter, depending on the context. This befits her status as an unmarried
        woman. When she goes to Damascus, she is the lady, as befits a wife and mother;
        she has entered the second stage of her life, and the term used to identify her
        shifts accordingly. In this line alone, she is identified as a wife. She has already
        wed the sultan and has given birth, but neither of these social milestones changed
        the poem's means of identifying her. However, here, as she plots with the priest,
        her status as the sultan's wife, as the falsely converted woman, is recalled. It is
        possible that the appellation is used for the sake of rhyme (*soudan's wiif–withouten
        striif*), but the flexibility and resourcefulness of Middle English poets, including
        The King of Tars poet, should not be underestimated. Tail-rhyme poetry is not
        easy to write, and the poet has yet to include tortured or failed rhymes; this
        supports the belief that this is a pointed choice and not just a convenient rhyme.

760–68 The poem's description of the baptism is minimal. Siobhan Bly Calkin notes
        that, "For late medieval theologians, what makes a Christian is the pronun-
        ciation of a specific verbal formula" that is absent in the poem ("Romance
        Baptisms," p. 106). Calkin further suggests that the absence of any formulaic
        language creates an emphasis on baptism as a means of building community.
        This is certainly important for the princess, who has to build a new, Christian
        community in Damas, beginning with her family.

763   *missomer tide*. Midsummer is a liminal time, the longest day of the year, and a pagan time of fecundity and conception. It celebrates the nativity of John the Baptist and is thus most fitting for the baptism of the child that Christ will transform, along with the conversion and translation of the sultan.

767–68   *And cleped it the name of Jon / In worthschip of the day*. The most likely candidate is John the Baptist, whose feast day is 24 June. John appears in all of the Gospels, but most importantly in Matthew 14:1–12 and Luke 1:5–25. The date was chosen because Luke 1:26 and 1:36 imply that John the Baptist was born six months earlier than Jesus.

769–77   The power of Christianity is proven through the princess's attempt to give her child form (see above, lines 600–18 and note for the deal she made with the sultan). The miracle is based on a fairly logical sequence of events: with baptism comes grace; with grace comes spiritual purity; and with spiritual purity comes physical purity and a single form, as the flesh imitates the soul. The child's heritage is no longer at odds with itself, as the Christian portion gains dominance.

772   *hide and flesche and fel*. "Hide" and "fel" are both terms for the skin. Although "hide" may refer to those portions that are covered in hair and "fel" those that are bare, it seems that the poet is using synonyms to amplify the new formation of the lump-child.

779   *teld . . . fore*. To "tellen fore" is to tell something forth, to tell in the presence of someone. Here, Cleophas is telling the sultan about the miracle of the child gaining form when baptized, but there is a sense of spreading a miracle, an important feature of hagiographic narratives that broadcast the good news. Relating this miracle will, as in many saints' lives, lead to the conversion of the listener (here, the sultan). See also note 1098.

783   *gold and purpel*. These two colors were associated with royalty. There is a further connotation of the East with purple, as the dye used for that color was found in Byzantium, whose emperors traditionally wore purple garments.

785   *joies five*. The importance of the five joys of the Virgin was as a means of guiding spiritual exercises. As Saupe notes, "Meditation on Mary's 'joys' recalls the events of Mary's life in terms of their spiritual significance," though the joys themselves varied slightly in different contexts and traditions (*Middle English Marian Lyrics*, p. 27). Saupe lists the joys in the Franciscan tradition as "the Annunciation, the Nativity, the Resurrection of Christ, the Ascension of Christ into heaven, and the Assumption of Mary into heaven," adding "sometimes the Epiphany (the visit of the Magi) is included and the Ascension omitted." Another, later poet, John the Blind Audelay, lists the five joys as the Nativity, Resurrection, Ascension, Assumption, and Coronation (*Poems and Carols*, ed. Fein, p. 282). Poems specifically celebrating the five joys were common; see, for example, Saupe, *Middle English Marian Lyrics*, poems 71–76 (pp. 137–46) and Audelay, "Prayer on the Joys of the Virgin" and Carol 18, "Joys of Mary" (*Poems and Carols*, ed. Fein, pp. 151 and 198–99, respectively). The five joys are also mentioned in *Sir Gawain and the Green Knight*, ed. Winny, lines 646–47, where they strengthen

Gawain's fortitude on the battlefield, for which reason he has the image of the Virgin on the inside of his shield.

793   *the soudan that was blac.* Despite hearing of the princess's white skin in the first stanza ("white as fether of swan," line 12), this is the first mention of the sultan's skin color, which suggests that it was not an important detail until now, in anticipation of his baptism and metamorphosis. Mentioning his skin color here also establishes a more clear dichotomy between the sultan and the princess, though he is not described as loathly, as are so many other foreign figures in medieval romance. See the note to lines 11–16 on the princess's beauty.

795   *With liif and limes and face.* The princess shows the sultan the child, which is no longer a lifeless lump of flesh, but a living being with human form. That form was instilled with baptism.

797   *nought worth the brostle of a swin.* Proverbial; see Whiting, *Proverbs, Sentences, and Proverbial Phrases* B552, which cites three texts present in Ak. Interestingly, the three citations all refer to the worthlessness of pagan gods. The first instance in Ak is this one, in *The King of Tars*; the next occurs in the couplet version of *Guy of Warwick*: "Thou sest Mahoun ne Apolin / Be nought worth the brestel of a swin" (*Guy of Warwick* [couplets], lines 3324–25); and the third appears in *Roland and Vernagu*:

> Rouland lough for that cri,
> And seyd "Mahoun sikerly
> No may thee help nought,
> No Jubiter, no Apolin,
> No is worth the brust of a swin,
> In hert no in thought."
> (lines 857–62)

The Ak texts are far from unique in ascribing worthlessness in such a manner, and the manuscript is not the origin of any of these three texts, so the common use of this proverb is striking. I have slightly modernized these quotations.

802   *bi Seyn Martin.* "One of the most popular saints of the Middle Ages" (Farmer, *Oxford Dictionary of Saints*, p. 333), Martin of Tours was famed for his generosity. Born c. 316 to a wealthy Roman family, Martin abandoned military service when he converted. Outside of Amiens, he cut his cloak in half to clothe a naked beggar. That night, he had a dream vision of Christ wearing the cloak, and Martin was baptized the next day. The first monk in Gaul (France), he founded the first monastery there before becoming bishop of Tours in 372. As bishop, he fostered the foundation of monasteries as a means of bringing Christianity to rural areas. After his death in 397, his life by Sulpicius Severus became a model of hagiography and was copied throughout the Middle Ages. Despite Martin's fame in Europe, Shores observes that he "appears to have been chosen for the sake of rhyme" (p. 210n802A). There is no clear connection between Martin's life and the events of the tale here, though the princess could obliquely refer to the divided cloak by saying "Yif the halvendel wer thin" (line 803). For a version of Martin's life, see Jacobus de Voragine, *Golden Legend*, pp. 663–74. In one of

the most interesting changes offered in the Vernon manuscript, the saint invoked at this point is not Martin, but Katherine of Alexandria. Katherine was a popular figure in Middle English literature, and her life appears in both the *Golden Legend* (pp. 708–16) and the *South English Legendary*, the latter of which is included in the Vernon but not in Ak. Such a substitution may indicate a different audience or simply the popularity of a different saint.

809–10   *Thou no hast no part theron ywis, / Noither of the child ne of me.* The princess severs her ties to the sultan here; as in lines 803–04, she disputes the sultan's role in creating the child, and she relies on the substitute father, God the Father, as a replacement the child gained with form in baptism. For more on medieval medical discourse and the role of baptism in giving form, see the introduction, pp. 14–16.

827–28   Although the sultan has already broken his idols in his fit of rage at their impotence (lines 646–57), here he promises to utterly destroy them as a sign of his conversion.

837–70   *Jhesu Cristes lay.* The princess briefly summarizes the Christian faith through these thirty-four lines, which mention both formal doctrine and popular belief. Although the miraculous transformation is a sign of God's power, this description of the tenets of Christianity completes the sultan's conversion. Convinced of the real power of Christianity, he learns the tenets of his new faith and abandons his old law in favor of the New Law.

844–46   Although the harrowing of Hell has no biblical testimony, it was a very popular story, as it logically explained the three days between the death and resurrection of Christ, and offered satisfaction (and hope) for the virtuous pagans and Jews (such as the patriarchs) who were barred from Heaven solely because they were born before the Incarnation. J. K. Elliott suggests the tale may have its origin in 1 Peter 3:19 ("in quo et his qui in carcere erant spiritibus veniens praedicavit" [Douay-Rheims: In which also coming he preached to those spirits that were in prison]), which "whetted the appetite of Christians for further information about this aspect of their early history" (*Apocryphal New Testament*, p. 165). This text is in the apocryphal Gospel of Nicodemus, written in Greek and translated into Latin and, from there, into many vernacular languages, including both Old and Middle English. The harrowing was elaborated quickly and circulated independently of the apocryphal gospel. Four manuscripts contain the Middle English text of the harrowing, including Ak (ff. ?35rb-?37rb or 37va stub). Knowledge of the story must have been widespread; David Bevington notes that it "forms an essential part of all the Corpus Christi cycles" (*Medieval Drama*, p. 594), a popular retelling of biblical tales presented in dramatic form throughout England. For an edition of the Ak *Harrowing*, see Hulme, *Middle-English Harrowing of Hell and Gospel of Nicodemus*, pp. 3–21. For a translation of the Greek and Latin texts of the Gospel of Nicodemus, see Elliott, *Apocryphal New Testament*, pp. 164–204.

856   *the crede.* Shores points out that it is unclear "to precisely which Creed the princess refers, for all of them speak of Christ's judgment of the living and the dead" (p. 211n856A). The two most likely are the Nicene Creed, used in the mass and

therefore familiar to the princess and the audience, or the Apostles' Creed, used at baptism, and equally appropriate here.

860   *And man arise fram ded to live*. A reference to the Final Judgment, when the dead shall rise from their graves and be judged. It also recalls the miraculous transformation of the child from a dead lump of flesh to a beautiful, well-formed, living boy.

867   *Erl, baroun, and bond*. A bond is a pledge, especially one which creates a feudal obligation; here, it refers specifically to the bondsman, contrasting the lowest rank in feudal society with two of the highest, earl and baron. The sense of this line is that all men should be judged according to their station.

876   *teche me Cristen lay*. Although lines 836–67 outline the basic theology of Christianity, there is little on living a Christian life. Here, the sultan asks for a fuller education, in keeping with his nascent conversion. His request for a priest should not be read as misogynist; the princess's description summarized Christ's life but discussed little else, while a priest would know the particulars of not only the Bible but also the other church doctrines a converted person would need to learn.

878   *bot we thre*. As before (line 260), the princess is part of a small group that has secret information that will transform the narrative: before, she and her parents were privy to her decision to wed the sultan, while here, only she, the sultan, and the priest are aware of the sultan's conversion.

906   *cristendom*. The primary meanings in *MED* focus on faith and doctrine; that is, Cleophas asks Christ to give the sultan strength to pursue his new faith.

919   *Cleophas*. Hornstein ("Study of Historical and Folk-lore Sources," chapter 2, esp. pp. 42–47) found some instances of a "Cleophas" in chronicles, though the distance between this poem and the historical record makes such a connection unlikely. Perryman suggests "perhaps a chronicle which associated a Cleophas with Tars had been seen by the author of the romance. More probably the historical associations are fortuitous since the name is likely to have been chosen for its symbolic allusion to St. Cleophas" (p. 113n925). The name "Cleophas" appears in two places in the Bible. First, Luke 24:18 identifies one of the travelers to Emmaus as "Cleophas"; he is the first of the travelers to speak to the risen Christ, and the name thus is appropriate for a priest who celebrates conversions in exile. The second instance is in John 19:25, where one of the three Marys present at the Crucifixion is named "Maria Cleopae"; she was thought to be either the wife or daughter of the traveler Cleophas. St. Cleophas was included in many fourteenth-century martyrologies, and the poet could have encountered the name in a religious context more readily than in a chronicle.

922–24   In one of the most commented-on passages of the poem, upon conversion to Christianity, the sultan's skin color changes from black to white. This is a visible sign of faith and the power of Christianity, the point being that the sultan now sees himself without blemish. There are parallel changes in *Cursor Mundi* (lines 8071–8122) and the *History of the Holy Rood-Tree* (ed. Napier, pp. 16, 17). Both relate the story of explicitly black Ethiopians who meet King David. When they pay proper respect to the rods that will become the cross, their skin color is changed from black to white, and the miracle converts them. It is worth recalling that there was no such change with the princess, as she did not truly convert, but simply appeared to follow her husband's faith. See the introduction, pp. 1–13, for more on the presentation of race in this poem.

935   *eyghen gray.* Grey eyes were a sign of rare beauty.

936–39 She now sees his spotless new self also.

942   *Hir joie gan wax al newe.* The princess was joyful at the child's transformation, and she specifically excluded the sultan from the family unit. When she sees the newly-baptized sultan, her joy increases because he has truly converted, and their family is complete. The phrase "al newe" also resonates with the theme of rebirth in the poem.

959   *thurth His sond.* "Message," as I have glossed *sond*, has a couple of possible meanings. The most obvious, of course, is the sultan's new metamorphosis from black to white, a visible message relaying the truth of Christianity through the purification of baptism. The Bible is also a strong possibility, as the sultan is newly aware of the message therein. In this poem, there are two other messages sent by Christ: first, the dream-vision, about which the sultan may know, and second, the lump-child's metamorphosis. Any of these (or all of them) could be the message he wants to relay to the king of Tars, each having played a part in the sultan's conversion.

979   It may be that Cleophas read the letter he brought aloud, especially if the letter is an open one, intended as a political document for the court as a whole rather than as a personal document from the sultan to his father-in-law. "Ywrought," line 980, is glossed "written," but could also mean "composed" or "prepared," and need not refer specifically to a written document. It is another instance of the tension between literacy and orality.

989   *honged opon a tre.* Christ, of course, was hung upon the tree, the cross, so it is interesting that the Saracens who will not convert will share a similar fate, just like many other saints and martyrs. It may be that those who will not convert are hanged by the neck, which is an ignominious ending generally reserved for traitors.

1002   *He schal hong and drawe.* Not quite the execution mentioned in line 989 ("honged opon a tre"), but in English law, hanging and drawing was an appropriate punishment for traitors, which the sultan clearly considers his men if they do not follow his orders and convert. However, given the centrality of faith to the poem, his order is a difficult proposition to accept simply. The princess's deceptive embrace of Islam shows that a religion must be entered willingly and with true belief, or the conversion is meaningless. The sultan needs a miracle to prove the veracity of Christianity, and the miracle is twofold: the shaping of his son and his own transformation from black to white skin. So why should the other lords covert, if they do not believe? They did not witness the transformation of either child or father. Rather than creating a mass conversion, this demand leads to a climactic battle between the forces of Christianity and Islam, characteristic of romance.

1004   *Erl, baroun, douk, and knight.* This set of four titles essentially covers the entirety of the English feudal hierarchy, excepting the king. The sultan is clearly asking the king of Tars to assemble an army consisting of his entire kingdom, as underscored in the next line: "Do alle your folk bide." The sultan recognizes the superior number of Saracens in his own kingdom, and wants to raise as large a force as he can to convert his people.

1006   *brini.* A *brini* is a coat of mail or hauberk. See also note 141, above.

1022   *knen.* This is an archaic plural of "knee," similar to the construction of "oxen" and "children," that has fallen out of use.

1027–38   After living in relative seclusion, the sultan finally presents himself to his people and announces his conversion. His skin color has changed, and it is possible that he has allowed the story of his son to circulate. Although he calls on his people to convert, rather than simply forcing them to do so, anyone who continues to follow the false law will be beheaded. He does seem to anticipate armed resistance, though, and waits for the king of Tars to arrive with his army. His expectation of violent resistance will be met and a war will follow, as the sultan and king of Tars fight five rebellious Saracen kings.

1032   *Ye mot ycristned be.* The sultan sincerely wishes to convert his people, with the might of the king of Tars supporting him. Although the sultan's army would surely be severely diminished, as some of his soldiers would not willingly convert, his forces will be augmented by the imprisoned Christian knights, like Sir Cleophas.

1036–37   This is the sultan's final attempt to convert his people peacefully. Those who do not renounce their faith and follow the sultan will be beheaded. This threat will be followed through in lines 1225–29.

1054–59   The sultan finally shows proper Christian charity, even though it is a little self-serving. He is generous with all his (Christian) prisoners, asking those who are able to fight to do so and giving food and medical aid to those who cannot.

1062   *In gest as so we rede.* Compare line 309. This is an oral formula that posits a "source" text, frequently appearing with small variations in romance literature. See *Amis and Amiloun* lines 144, 1546, 1729, and 2448; and *Stanzaic Guy of Warwick* line 216. The most common formula is "in romance as we rede" (see *Emaré* line 216; *Sir Launfal* line 741; *Sir Isumbras* line 759; *Octavian* lines 15, 282, and 1806; *Athelston* lines 383, 569, 623, and 779. Other variants include "in romans as men rede," (*Sir Gawain and the Carle of Carlisle*, line 51), "in chronicle for to rede" (*Siege of Milan*, line 9) and "in story as we rede" (*Tournament of Tottenham*, line 5).

1081–83   The five named heathen kings have long intrigued those scholars who wish to find historical connections and context for *The King of Tars*. Perryman believes they are just fictional names, carrying "no symbolic meaning" (p. 63), though she does draw some connections between these names and others in the texts that compose Ak (pp. 113n1087–114n1089). Shores, however, refers to her dissertation director's own dissertation, stating "The historicity of the five kings is discussed by Lillian Herlands Hornstein, 'A Study of the Historical and Folk-Lore Sources of the *King of Tars*,' unpubl. diss. (New York University, 1940), pp. 72f" (Shores, p. 212n1081–1083A, 997–999V). Though Hornstein's dissertation is interesting, the distance between historical figures and events and the texts in Ak may be too great to support specific connections or intentional resonances in this poem. Further, given the reality of variation in names, especially those that would be as unfamiliar to English scribes as Oriental names and titles, the original names of these figures, if they do have historical sources, are probably lost. These names are now used to emphasize their exotic nature.

1093   *Now herkneth to me bothe old and ying*. The poem here changes its expectations of the audience. It is no longer strictly a written text, but one that includes a call for the audience to pay attention. This evocation of oral performance recalls the poem's opening line. See the notes to line 554 and line 1062.

1098   *lithe*. *MED* defines *lithe* as synonymous with "listen," noting that "to lithen" is a "more or less empty metrical tag" (*lithen*, v.3, sense f). Here, it seems to be used for not only meter, but also amplification and as a refinement of the audience's participation. They are not only to listen, but to hear the story. See also note 1093. The emphasis adds to the importance of hearing as a means of participating in miracles. See also note 779.

1099   *Cristen soudan*. Although modern, secular readers will not see anything amiss here, the original audience would perceive this as a contradiction. Today, we read "sultan" as a social and political title and "Christian" as a religious and spiritual one, but medieval romance was less comfortable with such a strict division. Drawing on a number of works, especially romances, *MED* defines "soudan" primarily as a Moslem or Saracen leader; with such a strong connotation, a Christian sultan would appear to be an oxymoron.

1111   *Tabarie*. The identity of this name has a number of possibilities. Perryman observes "*Tabarie* may refer to a famous battlefield near the sea of Galilea . . . but it is common in romances as a Middle Eastern kingdom" (p. 114n1117). Like the names of the kings, it is likely just an exotic flourish, though there may be some connection to the brief romance "Hugh of Tabarie."

1121   *top seyl in the feld*. This phrase has been the subject of great speculation. Krause emends to "þat top *ouer* teyl in þe feld" ("Kleine Publicationen," line 1121). Bliss questions the emendation from Ak's "top seyl," suggesting a Middle English idiom "to overturn topsail to the earth," meaning "to fall head over heels" ("Notes on 'The King of Tars,'" p. 461). Shores and Perryman, following Bliss, both read "Þat, topseyl in þe feld" (Shores line 1121A, Perryman line 1127). However, the action may be described without reliance on a new idiom: the king of Tars takes Lesias's blow and "hit him (i.e., Lesias) so on the shield that the top [of it] flew into the field; he (the king of Tars) cast him (Lesias) down." Thus, Lesias needs to leap on a horse at the beginning of the next stanza.

1149   *with mayn.* This phrase means "with retainers" and "with strength," as in line 1187, the idiom "with might and mayn."

1166   *glaive.* *MED* describes a glaive as "a weapon with a long shaft ending in a point or an attached blade; lance, spear." The glaive suggested by the text here is more of a lance or spear, with which Clamadas strikes the sultan above the shield, that is, on his chest or head, nearly unhorsing him. See note to line 431 for more on the glaive.

1170   *houndes.* Although the Saracens have been metaphorically described as hounds throughout the text, by this point the word is almost devoid of any value, a commonplace descriptor to dehumanize the Saracens.

           fele. "Many," but it is tempting to read this as a scribal error for "fel" or "felle," which *MED* defines as "treacherous, deceitful, false; guileful, crafty; villainous, base; wicked, evil." However, it may be that the scribe or the original poet was interested in both senses, relying on the homonym.

1183–88   Memarok plays the role of the cowardly pagan here. A Christian hero or king would have been spurred on to greater deeds at the deaths of their allies, as are Arthur and Charlemagne. See, e.g., the *Alliterative Morte Arthure*, lines 2197–2217, and *The Song of Roland*, trans. Brault, lines 2987 and 3610–30. This further, if subtly, supports the correctness of Christianity — not only are the Christians infused with the power of God, but their enemies flee to live in dishonor rather than finishing the battle.

1200   *Wicke is thi servise.* Perryman describes two potential meanings for *servise* based on the *OED.* The line could mean "wicked is the reward for serving you" originating from *OED service,* sense 7 or "wicked is the condition of being your servant" coming from *OED service,* sense 1 (p. 114n1206). The passage as a whole remains the same either way: the Saracens recognize the impotency of their gods in the battle.

1202   *dreynt hem.* "Hem" is a reflexive pronoun: "they drowned themselves," describing the Saracens as a cowardly lot who would rather flee the battle than see their death in its conclusion; in the process, they drown as a result of the weight of their armor and equipment. Compare *The Song of Roland,* where Charlemagne traps the Moors between his army and the River Ebro:

> The pagans cry out to Tervagant, one of their gods,
> Then jump in, but they receive no protection.
> The men in full armor weigh the heaviest,
> Some go swirling down to the bottom;
> The others go floating downstream.
> The survivors, however, swallowed so much water;
> That they all drowned in fearful pain.
> (trans. Brault, lines 2468–74)

1218   *The bal up in the hode.* Perryman (p. 114n1224) notes this is an "unusual idiom" for the head, but that it is "particularly connected with the Auchinleck manuscript." She notes its appearance in *Arthour and Merlin,* line 394, and follows Bliss

("Notes on 'The King of Tars,'" p. 462), who observes its presence in sections of *King Alisaunder* and *Richard Coer de Lion* that are missing in Ak.

1225–29   The poem's casualness about the religious cleansing of Damas is disturbing. When the king and sultan claim victory for Christianity, they proceed to slay all those who did not convert, as the princess asked (lines 952–54) and the sultan threatened (lines 1036–38). Such religious cleansing echoes the desire of some crusaders to reclaim the Holy Land solely for Christians as well as the expulsion of the Jews from England by Edward I in 1290.

1230–41   Ak text ends abruptly on fol. 13vb. The opening of the next item in the gathering, "The Life of Adam and Eve," is also missing, which suggests that the lost section of *The King of Tars* is fairly short. "A precise estimate of what is lost is impossible, but it is probably no more than 40–60 lines" (Pearsall and Cunningham, introduction to *Auchinleck Manuscript*, p. xix). The final stanza is taken from the Vernon manuscript.

TEXTUAL NOTES

ABBREVIATIONS: MS: the Auchinleck Manuscript (base text); **P**: *The King of Tars*, ed. Perryman; **S**: *"The King of Tars*: A New Edition,"* ed. Shores; **V**: the Vernon Manuscript.

4	*Bituene.* So MS. S, P: *Bitvene.*
10	*hem bituen.* MS: *hem bitben.* S, P: *hem bitven.*
18	*proud and play.* So MS. V: *pert in play.* S, P: *proud [in] play*, but S notes MS reads *proud & play.*
35	*dou.* So MS. S, P: *don.*
38	*wrethe.* MS *wretþe.*
51	*bilive.* So MS. S, P: *bileve.*
79	*tak.* So MS, P. S: *take.*
94	*tille.* MS, S, P: *t[i]lle.*
95	*spille.* MS, S, P: *sp[i]lle.*
117	*mast.* So MS, S. P: *mest.*
121	*Lordings.* So MS. S, P: *Lordinges.*
131	*been.* So MS. S, P: *born.*
141	*helme, hauberk.* So MS. S: *helme [and] hauberk.* P: *helme [&] hauberk.*
147	*to.* So S, P. MS: *to to.*
148	*herd that.* MS: *herd sey þat*; *sey* is subpuncted for deletion. S: *herd sey þat.* P: *[it] herd þat*, with a note that *sey* is present and marked for deletion.
185	*stroke o.* So MS, S. P: *stroke of*, but the note in her apparatus reads *stroke o.*
205	*The.* MS: Initial *P* is two lines high; no paraph mark begins this stanza.
247	*Fader.* S, P: *F[a]der.* MS: *Fder.*
269	*me were slawe knightes thro.* So S, P. MS: *me slawe knightes thro were*, with *were* marked for insertion between *me* and *slawe.*
286	*letters.* So S, P. MS: *lettera.*
313	*The.* MS: *þ* is two lines high, with no paraph mark indicating the new stanza. S, P begin new stanza here.
335	*fro.* So MS, S. P: *from.*
353	*Her.* So MS, P. S: *Þer.*
354	P inserts three lines in brackets after line 354 to expand the short stanza to the standard twelve lines. The lines are based on V, but Perryman edited them to reflect the language present in MS:

> *Þai seye it miȝt non oþer go;*
> *Bitauȝten hir god for euermo*
> *& kist her douhter þare.* (p. 82)

81

362   *sounde.* So P, S. MS: *isounde*, with an interlinear correction to *sounde*.

370   MS: *N* is two lines high; no paraph.

381   *hethen.* MS, S: *heþþen.* P: *[heþen].*

402   *frende.* So S, P. MS: *frede.*

406   *war.* So MS, P. S: *was.*

430   *ywrought.* The *r* is an interlinear insertion.

440   *thurth.* So MS. S, P: *þurch.*

446   *Thurth.* So MS. S, P: *Þurch.*

451   *Ternagaunt.* So MS. S, P: *Teruagaunt.*

475   *Ternagant.* So MS. S, P: *Teruagant.*

477   *Empour.* So MS. S: *Emperour*, but she suggests MS is unclear. P: *Emperour.*

492   *sche was.* So S, P. MS: *sche was sche*; second "sche" marked for deletion.

499   S and P, following V, add "þer" at the end of the line to complete the rhyme.

500   *Ternagant.* So MS. S, P: *Teruagant.*

552   *Doukes, kinges.* So MS. S: *[Of] doukes [and] kinges.* P: *Doukes [&] kinges.*

554   *gest.* So P. MS: *grest.* S: *[wrest].*

573   *Thurth.* So MS. S, P: *Þurch.*

591   *thurth.* So MS. S, P: *þurch.*

595   *Ternagant.* So MS. S, P: *Teruagant.*

601   *bitwen.* MS: *bitben.* S, P: *bitven.*

625   *seyn.* So S, P. MS: *seyin*, with *i* marked for deletion.

626   *Ternagaunt.* So MS. S, P: *Teruagaunt.*

646   MS: *H* on three lines; no paraph.

655   *And.* So MS, S. P: *On*, but notes MS reads *And.*

         Ternagaunt. So MS, S, P: *Teruagaunt.*

724   *levedi seyd, "Artw a prest.* So P. S: *[seyd].* MS: *levedi artw a prest seyd* with insertion mark.

         Artw. So MS, S. P: *Art[o]w.*

734   *thi.* S: *þi.* MS: *þi*, marked for deletion. P omits.

739   *help in this stounde.* So MS, S. P: *help [& min], þis stounde[s].*

744   P includes three new lines to fill out the stanza, based on V:

         Her is a child selcouþe discriif.

         It haþ noiþer lim, no liif,

              No eyȝen for to se. (p. 93).

764   *Thurth.* So MS. S, P: *Þurch.*

766   *toke the flesche anon.* So S, P. MS: *toke flesche anon þe* with insertion mark.

784   *take.* So MS. S, P: *toke.*

785   *levedi with joies.* So S, P. MS: *levedi joies.*

794   *And sche schewed.* MS: *And schewed.* S, P: *[Sche] schewed.*

814   *Anon.* So MS, S. P: *[&] anon.*

818   *weren.* So MS. S, P: *were.*

830   *has to.* So MS. S, P: *has[t] to.* Geist suggests a scribal error conflated the final *t* of *hast* and the initial *t* of *to* ("Notes on 'The King of Tars,'" p. 178).

841	*blod*. S, P: *bl[o]d*. MS: *bld*.
874	*were*. So S, P. MS: *werer*.
905	*Thurth*. So MS. S, P: *Þurch*.
918	*baptize*. So MS, P. S: *baptiʒe*.
923	*thurth*. So MS. S, P: *þurch*.
953	*the*. So S, P. MS: *þen*.
959	*thurth*. So MS. S, P: *þurch*.
966	*Tars*. So S. P: *T[ar]s*. MS: *Tras*.
968	*thurth*. So MS. S, P: *þurch*.
970	*that*. So S, P. MS: *þat þat*.
973	*thurth*. So MS. S, P: *þurch*.
978	*Thurth*. So MS. S, P: *Þurch*.
1005	*folk bide*. MS: *bede folk*, with marks indicating transposition. S: *[folk] bede*. P: *folk bede*.
1013	*sexti*. So S, P. MS: *serti*.
1037	*erverichon*. So MS. S: *euerichon*. P: *[euerichon]*.
1072	*Ternagaunt*. So MS. S, P: *Teruagaunt*.
1089	*Ogein*. MS, S, P: *Oʒain*.
1093	*old*. So MS, S. P: *eld*.
1095	*drive*. So S. MS: *drrive*. P: *[driue]*.
1106	*bothe*. MS, S: *boþe*. P: *boþ*.
1118	*Lesias'*. MS, S, P: *Lessias*.
1130	*thurth*. So MS. S, P: *þurch*.
1134	*stounde*. So MS, S. P: *stound*.
1136	*To fight anon he was ful thro*. Supplied by P, based on V. MS omits. V, S read *To fihten anon he was ful þro*.
1139	*of*. S, P: *[so]*. MS omits.
1142	*Thurth*. So MS. S, P: *Þurch*.
1163	*thurth*. So MS. S, P: *þurch*.
	thurth the. MS has an erasure between these words, noted by S and P, who agree that two letters were erased.
1180	*thurth*. So MS. S, P: *þurch*.
1193	*fleyghe*. So MS, where it is marked for deletion. S: *fleyʒe*. P omits.
1210	*him*. So S, P. MS: *hin*.
1211	*he*. So P. MS: *hit*, possibly corrected to *he*. S: *he*, but notes "*e* unclear." P: *h[e]*.
1219	MS: No paraph.
1220	*Sarrains*. So MS, S. P: *sarra[ʒ]ins*.
1223	*men*. So MS, S. P: *man* (but notes manuscript reads *men*).
	he. MS: this pronoun is an interlinear insertion.
1226	*weren*. So MS, P. S: *werren*, but queries "The second *r* corrected from *e*?" (p. 198) P: *weren*, but notes "an *e*, possibly corrected to an *r*, occurs between *r* and *e*."
1230–41	Copied from V, as the Auchinleck manuscript has no ending.

APPENDIX:
VARIANT READINGS FROM THE VERNON MANUSCRIPT

There are three manuscripts that contain *The King of Tars*.[1] The differences in the two main witnesses, Auchinleck and Vernon, demonstrate the tendency and processes of scribal alteration very clearly.[2] Though they present the same tale, sharing episodes and structure, there are many lines that are vastly different. While the decision to base this text on Auchinleck is described in the introduction, some of the passages in Vernon are compelling for a number of reasons. In their introduction to *Bevis of Hampton*, Herzman, Drake, and Salisbury note "wide variation in manuscripts would certainly seem to be unusual, at least from the point of view of somewhat more 'canonical' texts — Biblical and classical — which were held in such awe by medieval authors that they dared not alter them."[3] Like *Bevis, The King of Tars* is an anonymous, roughly contemporary work that is "protected neither by sanctity nor sufficient authorial fame."[4] The antiquity of Auchinleck and its comparative completion has recommended it as closer to the original composition, and the unwritten assumption is that Vernon and Simeon were rewritten to be more in keeping with the desires of the patron; the language is "modernized," that is, made to better reflect contemporary usage and dialect, and some significant passages have been abbreviated or expanded. A complete list of all variant readings in the textual notes would essentially reproduce the text of Vernon; thus I have not included Vernon in the textual notes. However, as it is illustrative of medieval revision strategies to present a few passages for comparison, especially those which are unique to Vernon, I include them here.[5]

VERNON 1–4 (NO PARALLEL IN AUCHINLECK):

    Her biginneth of the kyng of Trars   *Here*
    And of the soudan of Dammas,
    Hou the soudan of Dammas
    Was icristned thoru Godus gras.   *baptized through*

---

[1] The three are Edinburgh, National Library of Scotland, Advocates' Library 19.2.1 (the Auchinleck manuscript); Oxford, Bodleian Library Poetry A.1 (the Vernon manuscript); and London, British Library Additional MS 22283 (the Simeon manuscript). See the introduction, pp. 16–20, for more information.

[2] A close comparison of Vernon and Simeon has revealed that Simeon is either a copy of Vernon or that they share the same exemplar. See Doyle, "Shaping of the Vernon and Simeon Manuscripts," for a more careful discussion of the relationship between the two.

[3] Herzman, Drake, and Salisbury, eds., *Four Romances of England*, p. 188.

[4] Herzman, Drake, and Salsibury, eds., *Four Romances of England*, p. 188.

[5] In keeping with the text, I have modernized those characters that have fallen out of use (e.g., thorn and yogh) that appear in the manuscript. I have also capitalized and added punctuation.

VERNON 76–84 (COMPARE AUCHINLECK 76–84):

Heo nolde not leeven on his maneers.   *She would not believe*
To God heo made hire preyers,
    That Lord Omnipotent,
And bad him take another thought.
80   For hire ne scholde he wedde nouht
      For gold, selver, ne rent.   *income*
Whon the messagers this herde seyn,
Soone thei tornede hem ageyn
    And to the soudan went.

VERNON 100–06 (COMPARE AUCHINLECK 100–06):

100   He tar the her of hed and berd   *tore; hair; head; beard*
And seide he wolde hir winne with swerd
    Beo his lord, Seynt Mahoun.   *By*
The table adoun riht he smot   *completely down; struck*
Into the flore foot-hot.   *immediately*
105   He lokede as a wylde lyon;
Al that he hitte he smot doun riht.

VERNON OMITS AUCHINLECK LINES 115 TO 120

VERNON 120–23 (COMPARE AUCHINLECK 126–29):

120   "And spouse hire with my ryng.   *wed*
And," he seide, withouten fayle,
"Arst he woulde me sle in batayle   *Before*
    And mony a gret lordying. . ."

VERNON OMITS AUCHINLECK LINES 139 TO 141

VERNON 145–75 (COMPARE AUCHINLECK 154–81):

145   Batayle thei sette uppon a day
Withinne the thridde day of May;
    No lengor nolde thei leende.   *would; linger*
The soudan com with gret power,
With helm briht and feir baneer,   *bright; fair banner*
150   Uppon that kyng to wende.   *go*

The soudan ladde an huge ost   *led; host (army)*
And com with muche pruyde and bost   *pride*
    With the kyng of Tars to fihte,
With hym mony a Sarazin feer.   *many; fierce*
155   Alle the feldes feor and neer   *fields far*
    Of helmes leomede lihte.   *With; gleamed bright*
The kyng of Tars com also
The soudan batayle for to do
    With mony a Cristene kniht.   *knight*

160 Eyther ost gon othur assayle;	*Either army began [to] assail [the] other*
Ther bigon a strong batayle	
That grislych was of siht.	*to see*
Threo hethene agein twey Cristene men	*Three; two*
And falde hem doun in the fen	
165 With wepnes stif and goode.	
The steorne Sarazins in that fiht	*fierce*
Slowe ur Cristene men doun riht;	*immediately*
Thei fouhte as heo weore woode.	*insane*
The soudan ost in that stounde	*sultan's army; moment*
170 Feolde the Cristene to the grounde,	*Knocked*
Mony a freoly foode.	*noble creature*
The Sarazins, withouten fayle,	
The Cristene culde in that batayle;	*killed*
Nas non that hem withstode.	*[There] was none who*
175 Whon the kyng of Tars sauh that siht. . .	

VERNON 181–86 (COMPARE AUCHINLECK 187–92):

The soudan neigh he hedde islawe	*nearly; slain*
But thritti thousent of hethene lawe	*thirty thousand*
Coomen him for to were	
And broughten him ageyn uppon his steede	*lifted; onto*
185 And holpe him wel in that nede	*helped*
That no mon mihte him dere.	*harm*

VERNON 204–22 (COMPARE AUCHINLECK 210–28):

Ur Cristene folk so fre	*Our; noble*
205 The Sarazins that tyme, saunz fayle,	*without*
Slowe ur Cristene in batayle.	
That reuthe hit was to se.	*calamity*
And on the morwe for heore sake	*And the next day for their*
Truwes thei gunne togidere take:	
210 A moneth and dayes thre.	
As the king of Tars sat in his halle,	
He made ful gret deol withalle	*sorrow*
For the folk that he hedde ilore.	*lost*
His douhter com in riche palle;	*fine cloth*
215 On kneos heo gon biforen him falle	*she*
And seide with syking sore:	*sighing*
"Fader," heo seide, "let me beo his wyf	*be*
That ther be no more strif	
Then hath ben her bifore.	*here*
220 For me hath be much folk schent,	*killed*

Slawen and morthred and torent,   *Slain; torn to pieces*
    Allas that I was bore!"

VERNON 230–46 (COMPARE AUCHINLECK 236–52):
230   "That Cristene men schul for me dye
        Thorw grace of God Almiht."   *Through*
    Then was the kyng of Tars ful wo,   *sad*
    Anon he onswerde tho
        To his douhter briht:

235   "Douhter," he seide, "blessed thou be
    Of God that sit in Trinité
        The tyme that thou were bore.   *born*
    That thou wolt save thi moder and me,
    Thi preyere now I graunte thee   *grant*
240   Of that thou bede before."   *asked*
    "Fader," heo seide, "par charité
    And for Crist in Trinité,
        Blyve that ich weore thore   *Quickly; there*
    Ar eny more serwe arere   *Before; sorrow arise*
245   That ye ne my moder dere   *[neither] you nor*
        For me beo nought forlore."

VERNON 277–82 (COMPARE AUCHINLECK 283–88):
    Whon the messagers thus herde seyn,
    Smartliche thei torned ageyn   *Quickly*
        To the soudan swart and wan.   *swarthy and dark*
280   Whon he herde heore lettres rad,   *heard; read*
    Then was he bothe blithe and glad   *happy*
        And murie as eny man.

VERNON OMITS AUCHINLECK LINES 288 TO 300

VERNON 297–315 (COMPARE AUCHINLECK 315–33):
    To the kyng of Tars he sent
    With Sarazins and with muche pryde   *great*
    With mony a juwel is nought to huyde   *conceal*
300   To make hym a present.
    Forth thei went that ilke tyde;   *same hour*
    To the kyng of Tars thei gan ryde
        That was bothe freo and gent   *noble and refined*
    Thei welcomed the messagere;
305   Of gret reuthe ye may here   *sadness*
        Whon thei to chaumbre went.

    In chaumbre kyng and qwene was tho,   *were then*
    In serwe and care and muche wo

For heore doughter hende.   *gentle*
310 Heor doughter com bifore hem wende   *went*
And bad hem bi hire counseil do
To save Cristene kende.
The doughter ther with wordes stille
Brought hem bothe in beter wille
315   And into halle gunne wende.   *began to go*

VERNON 325–31 (COMPARE AUCHINLECK 343–49):
325 The qwene onserde with mylde mod   *humble words*
To the messagers ther thei stod   *where*
And swor thenne anon riht,   *entirely at once*
"Ich fouchesaaf on him my blod   *promise*
To him heo nis not to good   *she; too*
330   Thaugh heo weore ten so briht."   *Even if she were ten [times] as beautiful (virtuous)*

The messagers weore glad and blythe

VERNON 335–43 (COMPARE AUCHINLECK 353–54):
335 Heore serwe couthe no mon kithe   *Their; could; reveal*
To seon hire from hem fare.   *go*
Thei seghe hit mihte non other go.   *no other [way] be*
The kyng and the qwene also;
Thei custe heore douhter thare,   *kissed*
340 Bitaughten hire God forever mo.   *Commended her [to]*
Hemself ageyn thei tornede tho
Of blisse thei weore al bare.   *were barren*

Now lete we of that mournyng

VERNON OMITS AUCHINLECK LINES 355 TO 370

VERNON 353–60 (COMPARE AUCHINLECK 380–87):
With riche clothes heo was cled   *In; dressed*
Hethene as thaugh heo ware.   *As if she were a heathen*

355 The soudan ther he sat in halle.
He comaundede his knihtes alle
That maiden for to fette.   *fetch*
In cloth of riche purpel palle,
And on hire hed a comeli calle,   *headdress*
360   Bi the soudan heo was sette.

VERNON 386–90 (COMPARE AUCHINLECK 413–17):
Knihtes and ladyes token heore rest;
Folk heo gonne withdrawe.   *[From] people she did withdraw*
The mayden nothing ne slepe   *slept not at all*

             But al niht lay and wepe
390   Forte that day gon dawe.   *Until*

VERNON 403–07 (COMPARE AUCHINLECK 430–34):
             So gryslich thei were wrought.
             Uche of hem a swerd brought
405   And mad hire afert so sore.   *sorely afraid*
             On Jhesu Crist was al hire thouht;
             Therfore thei mihte hire harme nouht.

VERNON 505–10 (COMPARE AUCHINLECK 532–37):
505   Heo leyden on as heo weore wode,   *They; mad*
             With swerdes and with maces goode,
                 Knihtes yonge and olde.
             So thei foughte with egre mood
             Of heore bodies ran the blod
510   In tale as hit is tolde.

VERNON OMITS AUCHINLECK LINES 550 TO 562

VERNON 559–62 (COMPARE AUCHINLECK 598–601):
             Then the ladi was ful wo.
560   Anon onswerde the soudan tho: *Quickly [she] replied to (answered) the sultan*
                 "Sire, let be thi thouht.
             The child that we have togedere two

VERNON 610–18 (COMPARE AUCHINLECK 649–51)
610   And leyde on til that he con swete   *began to*
             With sterne strokes and with grete:
                 On Jovyn and Plotoun,
             On Astrot and sire Jovin,
             On Tirmagaunt and Appolin,
615   He brak hem scolle and croun.
             On Tirmagaunt that was heore brother,
             He lafte no lyme hol with other,   *left; limb*
                 Ne on his lord Seynt Mahoun.

VERNON 679–86 (COMPARE AUCHINLECK 718–25):
             Adoun he fel uppon his kne
680   And feire he grette that ladi fre,   *noble*
                 And seide with sikynges sore
             And seide, "Dame, iblesset ye be
             Of God that sit in Trinité
                 The tyme that ye weore bore."
685   The ladi seide, "Art thou a prest?
             Beleevest thou on Jhesu Crist?
                 Const you of Cristes lore?"   *Know*

The prest onswerde soone anon
"*In verbo dei* ich was on   *By the word of God*
          Ten winter seththe and more."

Vernon 705–08 (compare Auchinleck 744):
705   "Al in priveté.
          Her is a child selcouth discrif,   *strange to look at*
          Hit nath nouther lyme ne lyf   *has not*
                    Ne eyen for to se."

Vernon 766–68 (compare Auchinleck 802–04):
          "Ye sire," heo seide, "be Seint Katerin,   *Katherine [of Alexandria]*
          Yif halvendel the child were thyn,
                    Then miht ye gladnes se."

Vernon omits Auchinleck line 811 to 13 and lines 823 to 70

Vernon 782–98 (compare Auchinleck 821–22, 871–82):
          To joye that lasteth withouten ende
                    May no mon hit discryve.   *describe*
          "Dame," seith the soudan, "beo nou stille.
785   Ichul ben at thin owne wille   *I will be*
                    And ben icristned blyve.   *baptized immediately*

          "Mi maumetrie ichul forsake   *idolatry*
          And Cristendom ichul take
                    Withinne this thridde day.
790   No more folk distruye I nil.
          I preye that prest to come me til
                    To teche me Cristene lay   *law*
          Priveliche, that hit be
          That no mon wite bote we thre
795   As ferforth as ye may.   *So far as*
          Yif eny hit wuste heigh or lowe,   *anyone; knew*
          Icholde be brent and don of dawe   *killed (done of days)*
                    Yif I forsoke my lay."   *law (faith)*

Vernon 829–34 (compare Auchinleck 913–18):
          The prest onswerde anon tho,
830   "Ichave al redi that schal therto
                    Al redi in alle wise."
          The soudan dihte him naked anon   *quickly made himself naked*
          Into the watur he con gon   *went*
                    And reseyvede the baptise.

Vernon 901–03 (compare Auchinleck 985–87):
          Priveliche with thin ost

Thou schouldest come withoute bost
And serche uche cuntray   *land*

VERNON 935–39 (COMPARE AUCHINLECK 1019–23):
935   A muri gretyng ther was gret   *merry; great*
             Of lordes that ther ware.
         A semely siht hit was to se: *pleasant; see*
         The ladi falde doun on kne   *fell*
             Bifore hire fader thare.

VERNON OMITS AUCHINLECK LINES 1066 TO 68

VERNON 985–91 (COMPARE AUCHINLECK 1072–75):
985   "Bi Mahoun and Tirmagaunt,
         No mon schal be heore waraunt,   *their guarantee*
             Weore thei nevere so stronge!"   *Though they be*
         Bothe soudan and kyng,
         And al that hem was folewyng,
990   The deth thei scholde afonge.   *receive*

         Fyf kynges were of heigh parayle

VERNON 1051–52 (COMPARE AUCHINLECK 1135–36):
         Kyng Merkel was ful wo;   *greatly sorry*
         To fihten anon he was ful thro.   *eager*

VERNON OMITS AUCHINLECK LINES 1160 TO 66

VERNON 1085–98 (COMPARE AUCHINLECK 1175–81):
1085 "That hethene dogge schal to grounde,
             Be the help of Seint Mihel.

         "I nul not dyghen in his dette.   *shall not die*
         A strok on hym ichul bisette   *bestow*
             Beo he never so bolde."
1090   Ur Ladi with an *Ave* he grette   *Our; Hail; greeted*
         That no mon scholde hym lette.   *hinder*
             The feendes strengthe to folde   *falter*
         He rod to hym anon ryht
         With a dunt of muche miht,   *blow*
1095   In stori as hit is tolde.
         He hutte him on the helm on hiht;
         Into the brayn thorw bacinet briht.   *through*
             Thus is his servyse yolde.

VERNON OMITS AUCHINLECK LINES 1194 TO 1229, BUT SUPPLIES AN ENDING, INCLUDED IN
THIS TEXT (LINES 1230–41).

 BIBLIOGRAPHY

Adams, George R., and Bernard S. Levy. "Good and Bad Fridays and May 3 in Chaucer." *English Language Notes* 3 (1966), 245–48.

Akbari, Suzanne Conklin. *Idols in the East: European Representations of Islam and the Orient, 1100–1400.* Ithaca, NY: Cornell University Press, 2009.

The Alliterative Morte Arthure. In Benson, pp. 129–284.

Amis and Amiloun. In Foster, pp. 1–74.

Athelston. In Herzman, Drake, and Salisbury, pp. 341–84.

The Auchinleck Manuscript: National Library of Scotland Advocates' MS. 19.2.1. Intro. Derek Pearsall and I. C. Cunningham. London: Scolar Press, 1979.

———. Ed. David Burnley and Alison Wiggins. National Library of Scotland. 5 July 2003. Online at http://auchinleck.nls.uk/.

Audelay, John the Blind. *Poems and Carols (Oxford, Bodleian Libary MS Douce 302).* Ed. Susanna Fein. Kalamazoo, MI: Medieval Institute Publications, 2009.

Baines, Anthony. *The Oxford Companion to Musical Instruments.* Oxford: Oxford University Press, 1992.

Benson, Larry, ed. *King Arthur's Death: The Middle English Stanzaic Morte Arthur and Alliterative Morte Arthure.* Rev. Edward E. Foster. Kalamazoo, MI: Medieval Institute Publications, 1994.

Bestiary: Being an English Version of the Bodleian Library, Oxford M. S. Bodley 764. Trans. Richard Barber. Woodbridge: Boydell Press, 1993.

Bevington, David, ed. *Medieval Drama.* Boston: Houghton Mifflin, 1975.

Bevis of Hampton. In Herzman, Drake, and Salisbury, pp. 187–340.

Blake, N. F. "Vernon MS: Contents and Organisation." In *Studies in The Vernon Manuscript.* Ed. Derek Pearsall. Cambridge: D. S. Brewer, 1990. Pp. 45–59.

Bliss, A. J. "Notes on 'The King of Tars.'" *Notes and Queries* 200 (1955), 461–62.

Boffey, Julia, and A. S. G. Edwards, eds. *A New Index of Middle English Verse.* London: British Library, 2005.

The Book of John Mandeville. Ed. Tamarah Kohanski and C. David Benson. Kalamazoo, MI: Medieval Institute Publications, 2007.

Braswell, Mary Flowers, ed. *Sir Perceval of Galles and Ywain and Gawain.* Kalamazoo, MI: Medieval Institute Publications, 1995.

Calkin, Siobhain Bly. "Marking Religion on the Body: Saracens, Categorization, and *The King of Tars.*" *The Journal of English and Germanic Philology* 104 (2005), 219–38.

———. *Saracens and the Making of English Identity: The Auchinleck Manuscript.* New York: Routledge, 2005.

———. "Romance Baptisms and Theological Contexts in *The King of Tars* and *Sir Ferumbras.*" In *Medieval Romance, Medieval Contexts.* Ed. Rhiannon Purdie and Michael Cichon. Cambridge: D. S. Brewer, 2011. Pp. 105–19.

Carter, Henry Holland. *A Dictionary of Middle English Musical Terms.* Bloomington: Indiana University Press, 1961.

Cary, George. *The Medieval Alexander.* Ed. D. J. A. Ross. New York: Garland Publishing, 1987.

Castleberry, Kristi. "Devils in the Bridal Chamber: Violent Unions in *The King of Tars*." In *Love, Friendship, Marriage*. Ed. Raffaele Florio and Aniesha R. Andrews. Weston, MA: The Public Heritage Institute at Regis College, 2012. Pp. 7–12.

Chaucer, Geoffrey. *The Riverside Chaucer*. Ed. Larry D. Benson. Boston: Houghton Mifflin, 1987.

Cohen, Jeffrey Jerome. "Monster Culture (Seven Theses)." In Cohen, ed., pp. 3–25.

———. "On Saracen Enjoyment: Some Fantasies of Race in Late Medieval France and England." *Journal of Medieval and Early Modern Studies* 31 (2001), 113–46.

———, ed. *Monster Theory: Reading Culture*. Minneapolis: University of Minnesota Press, 1996.

Cordery, Leona F. "A Medieval Interpretation of Risk: How Christian Women Deal with Adversity as Portrayed in *The Man of Law's Tale*, *Emaré*, and the *King of Tars*." In *The Self at Risk in English Literatures and Other Landscapes: Honoring Brigitte Scheer-Schäzler on the Occasion of Her 60ᵗʰ Birthday*. Ed. Gudrun M. Grabher and Sonja Bahn-Coblans. Innsbruck: Institut für Sprachwissenschaft der Universität Innsbruck, 1999. Pp. 177–85.

Correale, Robert M., and Mary Hamel, ed. *Sources and Analogues of The Canterbury Tales*. Vol 2. Cambridge: D. S. Brewer, 2005.

Cotterell, Arthur. *A Dictionary of World Mythology*. Oxford: Oxford University Press, 1986; rpt. 1990.

Crane, Susan. *Insular Romance: Politics, Faith, and Culture in Anglo-Norman and Middle English Literature*. Berkeley: University of California Press, 1986.

Cursor Mundi (The Cursur o the World). A Northumbrian Poem of the XIVth Century in Four Versions. Ed. Richard Morris. EETS o.s. 57, 59, 62, 66, 68, 99, 101. London: K. Paul, Trench, Trübner & Co., 1874–93; rpt. London, New York: Oxford University Press, 1961–66.

Czarnowus, Anna. "'Stille as Ston': Oriental Deformity in *The King of Tars*." *Studia Anglica Posnaniensia* 44 (2008), 463–74.

The Debate of the Body and the Soul. See *Þe Desputisoun Bitwen Þe Bodi and Þe Soule*.

Þe Desputisoun Bitwen Þe Bodi and Þe Soule. Ed. Wilhelm Linow. Amsterdam: Rodopi, 1970.

Doyle, A. I. "The Shaping of the Vernon and Simeon Manuscripts." In *Chaucer and Middle English Studies in Honour of Rossell Hope Robbins*. Ed. Beryl Rowland. Kent, OH: George Allen & Unwin, 1974. Pp. 328–41.

———. "Introduction." In *The Vernon Manuscript: A Facsimile of Bodleian Library, Oxford, MS. Eng. poet. a.1*. Cambridge: D. S. Brewer, 1987. Pp. 1–16.

Elliott, J. K. *The Apocryphal New Testament: A Collection of Apocryphal Christian Literature in an English Translation*. Oxford: Clarendon Press, 1993.

Ellzey, Mary. "The Advice of Wives in Three Middle English Romances: *The King of Tars*, *Sir Cleges*, and *Athelston*." *Medieval Perspectives* 7 (1992), 44–52.

Emaré. In Laskaya and Salisbury, pp. 145–99.

Farmer, David Hugh. *The Oxford Dictionary of Saints*. Fourth edition. Oxford: Oxford University Press, 1997.

Forni, Kathleen, ed. *The Chaucerian Apocrypha: A Selection*. Kalamazoo, MI: Medieval Institute Publications, 2005.

Foster, Edward E., ed. *Amis and Amiloun, Robert of Cisyle, and Sir Amadace*. Second edition. Kalamazoo, MI: Medieval Institute Publications, 2007.

Friedman, John Block. *The Monstrous Races in Medieval Art and Thought*. Cambridge, MA: Harvard University Press, 1981.

Geist, Robert J., ed. See *The King of Tars*.

———. "On the Genesis of 'The King of Tars.'" *Journal of English and Germanic Philology* 42 (1943), 260–68.

———. "Notes on 'The King of Tars.'" *Journal of English and Germanic Philology* 47 (1948), 173–78.

Geoffrey of Monmouth. *The History of the Kings of Britain*. Trans. Lewis Thorpe. Harmondsworth: Penguin, 1966.

Gerritsen, Willem P., and Anthony G. van Melle, eds. *A Dictionary of Medieval Heroes: Characters in Medieval Narrative Traditions and Their Afterlife in Literature, Theatre and the Visual Arts*. Trans. Tanis Guest. Woodbridge: The Boydell Press, 1998.

Gibson, Angela L. "Fictions of Abduction in the Auchinleck Manuscript, the Pearl Poet, Chaucer, and Malory." Ph.D. Diss., University of Rochester, 2007.

Gilbert, Jane. "Unnatural Mothers and Monstrous Children in *The King of Tars* and *Sir Gowther*." In *Medieval Women: Texts and Contexts in Late Medieval Britain: Essays for Felicity Riddy*. Ed. Jocelyn Wogan-Browne, Rosalynn Voaden, Arlyn Diamond, Ann Hutchison, Carol M. Meale, and Lesley Johnson. Turnhout: Brepols, 2000. Pp. 329–44.

———. "Putting the Pulp into Fiction: The Lump-Child and Its Parents in *The King of Tars*." In *Pulp Fictions of Medieval England: Essays in Popular Romance*. Ed. Nicola McDonald. Manchester: Manchester University Press, 2004. Pp. 102–23.

Gower, John. *Confessio Amantis*. Ed. Russell A. Peck, with Latin translations by Andrew Galloway. 3 vols. Kalamazoo, MI: Medieval Institute Publications, 2000–06.

"Guy of Warwick (couplets)." *The Auchinleck Manuscript*. Ed. Burnley and Wiggins. 5 July 2003. Online at http://auchinleck.nls.uk/mss/guy_cp.html.

Hahn, Thomas. "The Difference the Middle Ages Makes: Color and Race before the Modern World." *Journal of Medieval and Early Modern Studies* 31 (2001), 1–37.

———, ed. *Sir Gawain: Eleven Romances and Tales*. Kalamazoo, MI: Medieval Institute Publications, 1995.

Hanna, Ralph. "Reconsidering the Auchinleck Manuscript." In *New Directions in Later Medieval Manuscript Studies: Essays from the 1998 Harvard Conference*. Ed. Derek Pearsall. Woodbridge: York Medieval Press, 2000. Pp. 91–102.

Havelok the Dane. In Herzman, Drake, and Salisbury, pp. 72–185.

Heng, Geraldine. *Empire of Magic: Medieval Romance and the Politics of Cultural Fantasy*. New York: Columbia University Press, 2003.

Henryson, Robert. *The Complete Poems of Robert Henryson*. Ed. David J. Parkinson. Kalamazoo, MI: Medieval Institute Publications, 2010.

Herzman, Ronald B., Graham Drake, and Eve Salisbury, eds. *Four Romances of England: King Horn, Havelok the Dane, Bevis of Hampton, Athelston*. Kalamazoo, MI: Medieval Institute Publications, 1999.

Hibbard, Laura A. *Mediæval Romance in England: A Study of the Sources and Analogues of the Non-Cyclic Metrical Romances*. New York: Oxford University Press, 1924; rpt. New York: Burt Franklin, 1960.

Hilton, Walter. *The Scale of Perfection*. Ed. Thomas H. Bestul. Kalamazoo, MI: Medieval Institute Publications, 2000.

Hornstein, Lilian Herlands. "A Study of Historical and Folk-lore Sources of *The King of Tars*." Ph.D. Diss., New York University, 1939.

———. "Trivet's Constance and the *King of Tars*." *Modern Language Notes* 55 (1940), 354–57.

———. "A Folklore Theme in *The King of Tars*." *Philological Quarterly* 20 (1941), 82–87.

———. "The Historical Background of *The King of Tars*." *Speculum* 16 (1941), 404–14.

———. "New Analogues to 'The King of Tars.'" *Modern Language Review* 36 (1941), 433–42.

Hudson, Harriet, ed. *Four Middle English Romances: Sir Isumbras, Octavian, Sir Eglamour of Artois, Sir Tryamour*. Second edition. Kalamazoo, MI: Medieval Institute Publications, 2006.

Hulme, William Henry, ed. *The Middle-English Harrowing of Hell and Gospel of Nicodemus*. EETS e.s. 100. London: Oxford University Press 1907; rpt. Milwood, NY: Kraus Reprint, 1991.

Jacobus de Voragine. *The Golden Legend*. Trans. Granger Ryan and Helmut Ripperger. New York: Arno Press, 1969.

The King of Tars.

———. Ed. Thomas Warton as "The King of Tars." In *The History of English Poetry, from the Close of the Eleventh to the Commencement of the Eighteenth Century*. 3 vols. London: J. Dodsley; J. Walter; T. Becket; J. Robson; G. Robinson, and J. Bew, 1774. 1:190–97.

———. Ed. Joseph Ritson as "The Kyng of Tars; and the Soudan of Dammas." In *Ancient Engleish Metrical Romanceës*. 2 vols. London: W. Bulmer and Company, 1802. 2:156–203.

———. Ed. F. Krause as "Kleine Publicationen aus der Auchinleck-hs, IX: *The King of Tars*." *Englische Studien* 11 (1888), 1–62.

———. Ed. Robert J. Geist as "*The King of Tars*: A Medieval Romance." Ph.D. Diss., University of Illinois, Urbana-Champaign, 1940.

———. Ed. Doris Shores as "*The King of Tars*: A New Edition." Ph.D. Diss., New York University, 1969.

———. Ed. Judith Perryman as *The King of Tars: Ed. from the Auchinleck MS, Advocates 19.2.1*. Heidelberg: Carl Winter, 1980.

Kooper, Erik, ed. *Sentimental and Humorous Romances: Floris and Blancheflour, Sir Degrevant, The Squire of Low Degree, The Tournament of Tottenham, and The Feast of Tottenham*. Kalamazoo, MI: Medieval Institute Publications, 2006.

Krause, F. See *The King of Tars*.

Langland, William. *The Vision of Piers Plowman: A Critical Edition of the B-Text Based on Trinity College Cambridge MS B.15.17*. Second edition. Ed. A. V. C. Schmidt. London: Everyman, 1995.

Laskaya, Anne and Eve Salisbury, eds. *The Middle English Breton Lays*. Revised edition. Kalamazoo, MI: Medieval Institute Publications, 2001.

Loomis, Laura Hibbard. "Chaucer and the Auchinleck MS: 'Thopas' and 'Guy of Warwick.'" In *Essays and Studies in Honor of Carleton Brown*. New York: New York University Press, 1940. Pp. 111–28.

———. "The Auchinleck Manuscript and a Possible London Bookshop of 1330–1340." *PMLA* 57 (1942), 595–627.

Lupack, Alan, ed. *Three Middle English Charlemagne Romances: The Sultan of Babylon, The Siege of Milan, and The Tale of Ralph the Collier*. Kalamazoo, MI: Medieval Institute Publications, 1990.

McCall, John P. "Chaucer's May 3." *Modern Language Notes* 76 (1961), 201–05.

Mehl, Dieter. *The Middle English Romances of the Thirteenth and Fourteenth Centuries*. London: Routledge & Kegan Paul, 1969.

Metlitzki, Dorothee. *The Matter of Araby in Medieval England*. New Haven, CT: Yale University Press, 1977.

Napier, Arthur S., ed. *History of the Holy Rood-tree, a Twelfth Century Version of the Cross-Legend, with Notes on the Orthography of the Ormulum and a Middle English Compassio Mariae*. EETS o.s. 103. London: Kegan Paul, Trench, Trübner & Co., 1894.

Nicolle, David. *Medieval Warfare Source Book*. Vol. 1: Warfare in Western Christendom. London: Arms and Armour Press, 1995.

Octavian. In Hudson, pp. 39–95.

"On the Seven Deadly Sins." *The Auchinleck Manuscript*. Ed. Burnley and Wiggins. 5 July 2003. Online at http://auchinleck.nls.uk/mss/sins.html.

Orchard, Andy. *Pride and Prodigies: Studies in the Monsters of the* Beowulf-*Manuscript*. Toronto: University of Toronto Press, 2003.

Peck, Russell A. "Numerology and Chaucer's *Troilus and Criseyde*." *Mosaic* 5.4 (1972), 1–29.

Perryman, Judith. See *The King of Tars*.

Pickering, Oliver. "Stanzaic Verse in the Auchinleck Manuscript: *The Alphabetical Praise of Women*." In *Studies in Late Medieval and Early Renaissance Texts in Honour of John Scattergood*. Ed. Anne Marie D'Arcy and Alan J. Fletcher. Dublin: Four Courts Press, 2005. Pp. 287–304.

Purdie, Rhiannon. *Anglicising Romance: Tail-rhyme and Genre in Medieval English Literature*. Woodbridge: D. S. Brewer, 2008.

Ritson, Joseph. See *The King of Tars*.

"Roland and Vernagu." *The Auchinleck Manuscript*. Ed. Burnley and Wiggins. 5 July 2003. Online at http://auchinleck.nls.uk/mss/roland.html.

Rubin, Miri. *Mother of God: A History of the Virgin Mary*. New Haven, CT: Yale University Press, 2009.

Salisbury, Eve, ed. *The Trials and Joys of Marriage*. Kalamazoo, MI: Medieval Institute Publications, 2002.

Saunders, Corinne. *Magic and the Supernatural in Medieval English Romance*. Cambridge: D. S. Brewer, 2010.

Saunders, J. J. *A History of Medieval Islam*. London: Routledge, 1965.

Saupe, Karen, ed. *Middle English Marian Lyrics*. Kalamazoo, MI: Medieval Institute Publications, 1998.

Shakespeare, William. *Hamlet*. Ed. Harold Jenkins. London: Methuen, 1982.

Shonk, Timothy A. "A Study of the Auchinleck Manuscript: Bookmen and Bookmaking in the Early Fourteenth Century." *Speculum* 60 (1985), 71–91.

———. "A Study of the Auchinleck Manuscript: Investigations into the Processes of Book Making in the Fourteenth Century." Ph.D. Diss., University of Tennessee, 1985.

Shores, Doris. See *The King of Tars*.

The Siege of Milan. In Lupack, pp. 105–60.

Sir Gawain and the Carle of Carlisle. In Hahn, ed., pp. 112.

Sir Gawain and the Green Knight: Middle English Text with Facing Translation. Ed. James Winny. Peterborough: Broadview Press, 1992.

Sir Gawain and the Green Knight: A Verse Translation. Trans. Keith Harrison. Oxford: Oxford University Press, 1983.

Sir Gowther. In Laskaya and Salisbury, pp. 263–307.

Sir Isumbras. In Hudson, pp. 5–38.

Sir Launfal. In Laskaya and Salisbury, pp. 201–62.

Sir Tristrem. In *Lancelot of the Laik and Sir Tristrem*. Ed. Alan Lupack. Kalamazoo, MI: Medieval Institute Publications, 1994. Pp. 143–277.

Solomon, Stanley J. *Beyond Formula: American Film Genres*. San Diego, CA: Harcourt Brace Jovanovich, 1976.

The Song of Roland: An Analytical Edition. 2 vols. Trans. Gerard J. Brault. University Park: Pennsylvania State University Press, 1978.

Stanzaic Guy of Warwick. Ed. Alison Wiggins. Kalamazoo, MI: Medieval Institute Publications, 2004.

Strickland, Debra Higgs. *Saracens, Demons, and Jews: Making Monsters in Medieval Art*. Princeton, NJ: Princeton University Press, 2003.

The Sultan of Babylon. In Lupack, pp. 1–103.

Symes, Carol. "Manuscript Matrix, Modern Canon." In *Middle English*. Ed. Paul Strohm. Oxford: Oxford University Press, 2007. Pp. 7–22.

The Tale of Ralph the Collier. In Lupack, pp. 161–204.

The Tournament of Tottenham. In Kooper, pp. 181–204.

Trevet, Nicholas. In Correale and Hamel, pp. 277–350.

Turville-Petre, Thorlac. *England the Nation: Language, Literature, and National Identity, 1290–1340*. Oxford: Clarendon Press, 1996.

Tyerman, Christopher. *England and the Crusades: 1095–1588*. Chicago: University of Chicago Press, 1988.

———. *God's War: A New History of the Crusades*. Cambridge, MA: Belknap Press, 2006.

Uebel, Michael. "Unthinking the Monster: Twelfth-Century Responses to Saracen Alterity." In Cohen, ed., pp. 264–91.

The Vernon Manuscript: A Facsimile of Bodleian Library, Oxford, MS. Eng. poet. a.1. Intro. A. I. Doyle. Cambridge: D. S. Brewer, 1987.

Warton, Thomas. See *The King of Tars*.

Whiting, Bartlett Jere, with the collaboration of Helen Wescott Whiting. *Proverbs, Sentences, and Proverbial Phrases from English Writings Mainly before 1500*. Cambridge, MA: Belknap Press, 1968.

Wiggins, Alison. "The Auchinleck Manuscript: Importance." *The Auchinleck Manuscript*. Ed. Burnley and Wiggins. 5 July 2003. Online at http://auchinleck.nls.uk/editorial/importance.html.

Williams, David. *Deformed Discourse: The Function of the Monster in Mediaeval Thought and Literature*. Montreal: McGill-Queen's University Press, 1996.

Winstead, Karen A. "Saints, Wives, and Other 'Hooly Thynges': Pious Laywomen in Middle English Romance." *Chaucer Yearbook* 2 (1995), 137–54.

Wolfram von Eschenbach. *Parzival*. Trans. Helen M. Mustard and Charles E. Passage. New York: Vintage Books, 1961.

Woolf, Rosemary. "The Theme of Christ the Lover-Knight in Medieval English Literature." *The Review of English Studies*, New Series 13 (1962), 1–16.

GLOSSARY

abide *remain, linger*

ac *but*

aferd *afraid*

afin *thoroughly*

amorwe *on the next day*

anon *at once, immediately*

aplight *assuredly, in truth, indeed*

aqueld *killed, destroyed*

ar *before*

arere *arise*

aright (adj.) *proper*; (adv.) *properly*

arliche *early*

arst *first, rather*

artw *are you*

asay *test, try*

astow *as you*

atreyd *betrayed*

auter *altar*

aventours *adventures, experiences*

bateyl(e) *battle*

bede *bade, offered*

bende *bonds, fetters*

bide *ask, beg, plead for*

biment *bemoaned*

bird *lady, maiden*

bispac *announced, spoke out*

bituene *between*

ble *complexion, appearance*

blithe (adj.) *happy*; (adv.) *happily*

blive *quickly*

bore *born*

bot (n.) *good, help, remedy*; (prep.) *unless*

brac *broke*

brend, brent *burned*

breyd *jerk, sudden movement; moment, short space of time*

brini *chainmail coat*

brosten *burst*

canstow *do you know*

chere *appearance, behavior*

clef *cleaved*

cleped *called*

conseyle *advise*

couthe *could, was able*

cristen (v.) *baptize*; (adj.) *Christian*

cuntek *violence*

dede *did*

deme *judge*

derd *did wrong, harmed*

develen *devils*

dight *make ready, prepare*

diol *sadness*

do *do; cause (causative aspect)*

dome *judgment*

drake *dragon*

dreye *endure*

drough *dragged, pulled, drew*

duhti *powerful*

durst *dared*

eke *also*

fader *father*

fare *travel*

fas *face*

fauchoun *curved sword; falchion*

fawe *eagerly, gladly, willingly*

feir (adj.) *fair, beautiful*; (adv.) *pleasantly, politely*

fel (n.) *skin*; (adj.) *evil, treacherous, crafty*

felawerede *company, community*

fele *many*
felle *end*
fendes *fiends*
fer *fierce, bold; far*
ferd (adj.) *afraid;* (v.) *appeared, seemed; wandered*
fere *companions, company*
ferred *community, company*
fers *fierce, bold*
fett *fetch*
fleighe, fleyghe, fleye *flew*
fo *foe*
forlore *lost*
forthi *therefore*
fousoun *abundance*
fram *from*
fre *free, noble*

gaf *gave*
game *sport*
gan *began; did* (causative aspect)
gede *went*
gent *gentle*
gere *go*
gest *poem, tale*
geten *begotten*
gif, gaf *give, gave*
gode *good*
gras *grace*
graunt *grant*
grede *to cry out*
grimli *grim, savage*

hali *holy*
halwed *sanctified*
hele *heal*
hem *them*
hende *courteous, pleasant; skillful; well-bred*
hendeliche *courteously, pleasantly*
hent *held, raised*
heo *she*
her *their*
herken, herkneth *listen*
hest *behest, command*
hete *are named*
heteliche *violently*

heved *head*
heveded *beheaded*
heye (v.) *hasten, hurry;* (adj.) *high, important*
hider *here*
hight *was called*
hond *hand*
hos *hoarse*
hou *how*

ich (adj.) *each, every;* (pron.) *I*
ichave *I have*
ichil *I will*
ichon *each one*

kende *kind, species; nature*
kene *bold, brave, keen*
kithe *describe, know; demonstrate*
knawe *know*

lasse *lesser*
lat, lete, leten *allow; omit; abandon; leave; allow to pass*
lay *law, religion*
leche *physician*
lede *people*
lemed *gleamed, shone*
lende *remain, stay, tarry*
leng *longer; long*
lere *learn*
lesing *lying*
leten see **lat**
lett *hinder, prevent; delay, tarry*
leve (v.) *believe;* (adj.) *dear*
levedi *lady*
light *alit*
lime *limb*
live *life*
liver *deliver*
los *fame*
lothliche *loathly, ugly*

maked *made*
mare *greater*
maumettes *idols*
may *maiden*
meistri *force, power*

mete *food*
mett *mate, spouse*
meyné *force, power*
meyne *retainers*
michel *great, much*
miri *merry*
mis *error*
missomer *midsummer*
mode *mood, mind, heart, disposition*
mon *prayer*
morwe *morning*
mot *may, must*
mounde *prowess*

nam *became; took*
neghe *almost, nearly*
ner *nearly*
neye *nearly*
neyghe *to approach*
no . . . no *neither . . . nor*
nold *would not*

odoun *down*
ofweved *struck off*
ogein *against*
olive *alive*
onest *seemly, magnificent*
orouwe *in a row*
ost *host; eucharist*
oway *away*

palle *fine cloth*
par charité *by (for) charity, by (for) the love of God*
pers *peers*
pleyner *complete*
pousté *power*
preier *prayer*
priked *spurred*
privité *secrecy*

quite *completely, entirely*

real *regal*
rede *advice*
redi (adj.) *ready, prepared*; (adv.) *completely*

reweful, reweli *dismal, pitiful*
rewthe *compassion, pity; calamity, misfortune*
richliche *richly*
right (adj.) *right; just, straight*; (adv.) *completely*
rime *poem*
rode *complexion; rood, cross*
ros *rose*
rout *company, gang*

samned *assembled*
Sarrazin *Saracen*
sawe *saying, speech*
scast *chaste*
schent *killed*
schewe *show*
selcouthe *rare, strange, wonderful*
selve *very*
semly *seemly, pleasant*
sen *see*
sett *set, raised*
seyn *saint*
siked *sighed*
sithe *time*
slawe *slain*
slough *slew*
so *so, as, as if, like*
sond *message, messenger*
soudan *sultan*
spac *spoke*
stede *place; horse*
steven *voice*
steye *ascended, mounted*
stithe *strong, powerful*
stounde *moment, time*
stout *fierce, proud, strong*
swevening *swoon*
swiche *such*
swin *pig*
swithe *quickly*

tan *taken*
tharf *need*
thede *countries, nations, people*
thei *though*
ther *there, where*

therto *also, in addition; in this, to this*
tho (pron.) *those*; (adv.) *then*
tholed *suffered*
thritti *thirty*
thro *eager, zealous; excellent, worthy*
thurth *through*
tide *time, hour, season*
tille *to*
tint *wasted*
tocleved *split apart*
todrive, todreved *scatter(ed)*
toke *took*
tre *tree (cross)*

unride *fierce, savage; monstrous; large, great; numerous*

vertu *virtue*

wald *desire, wish, intend*
waraunt *defender*
wend(e) *go, depart*
wene (n.) *doubt*

wer *war*
wight *man, human*
wightike *vigorously*
wild *desired, wished, intended*
wille *desire, disposition*
wiman *woman*
wist *knew*
wite (v.) *know, think, ask; believe, understand*
wode *mad, insane*
wond *hesitate*
worthschip *honor*
wreche *affliction*
wrethe *wrath, anger*
wrothe *angry*

Y *I*
yfere *together*
yif *if*
yplight *indeed*
yradde *read*
ysame *together*
ywis *indeed, truly*

✎ MIDDLE ENGLISH TEXTS SERIES

The Floure and the Leafe, The Assembly of Ladies, The Isle of Ladies, edited by Derek Pearsall (1990)

Three Middle English Charlemagne Romances, edited by Alan Lupack (1990)

Six Ecclesiastical Satires, edited by James M. Dean (1991)

Heroic Women from the Old Testament in Middle English Verse, edited by Russell A. Peck (1991)

The Canterbury Tales: Fifteenth-Century Continuations and Additions, edited by John M. Bowers (1992)

Gavin Douglas, *The Palis of Honoure*, edited by David Parkinson (1992)

Wynnere and Wastoure and The Parlement of the Thre Ages, edited by Warren Ginsberg (1992)

The Shewings of Julian of Norwich, edited by Georgia Ronan Crampton (1994)

King Arthur's Death: The Middle English Stanzaic Morte Arthur and Alliterative Morte Arthure, edited by Larry D. Benson, revised by Edward E. Foster (1994)

Lancelot of the Laik and Sir Tristrem, edited by Alan Lupack (1994)

Sir Gawain: Eleven Romances and Tales, edited by Thomas Hahn (1995)

The Middle English Breton Lays, edited by Anne Laskaya and Eve Salisbury (1995)

Sir Perceval of Galles and Ywain and Gawain, edited by Mary Flowers Braswell (1995)

Four Middle English Romances: Sir Isumbras, Octavian, Sir Eglamour of Artois, Sir Tryamour, edited by Harriet Hudson (1996; second edition 2006)

The Poems of Laurence Minot, 1333–1352, edited by Richard H. Osberg (1996)

Medieval English Political Writings, edited by James M. Dean (1996)

The Book of Margery Kempe, edited by Lynn Staley (1996)

Amis and Amiloun, Robert of Cisyle, and Sir Amadace, edited by Edward E. Foster (1997; second edition 2007)

The Cloud of Unknowing, edited by Patrick J. Gallacher (1997)

Robin Hood and Other Outlaw Tales, edited by Stephen Knight and Thomas Ohlgren (1997; second edition 2000)

The Poems of Robert Henryson, edited by Robert L. Kindrick with the assistance of Kristie A. Bixby (1997)

Moral Love Songs and Laments, edited by Susanna Greer Fein (1998)

John Lydgate, *Troy Book Selections*, edited by Robert R. Edwards (1998)

Thomas Usk, *The Testament of Love*, edited by R. Allen Shoaf (1998)

Prose Merlin, edited by John Conlee (1998)

Middle English Marian Lyrics, edited by Karen Saupe (1998)

John Metham, *Amoryus and Cleopes*, edited by Stephen F. Page (1999)

Four Romances of England: King Horn, Havelok the Dane, Bevis of Hampton, Athelston, edited by Ronald B. Herzman, Graham Drake, and Eve Salisbury (1999)

The Assembly of Gods: Le Assemble de Dyeus, or Banquet of Gods and Goddesses, with the Discourse of Reason and Sensuality, edited by Jane Chance (1999)

Thomas Hoccleve, *The Regiment of Princes*, edited by Charles R. Blyth (1999)

John Capgrave, *The Life of Saint Katherine*, edited by Karen A. Winstead (1999)

John Gower, *Confessio Amantis*, Vol. 1, edited by Russell A. Peck; with Latin translations by Andrew Galloway (2000; second edition 2006); Vol. 2 (2003; second edition 2013); Vol. 3 (2004)

Richard the Redeless and Mum and the Sothsegger, edited by James M. Dean (2000)

Ancrene Wisse, edited by Robert Hasenfratz (2000)

Walter Hilton, *The Scale of Perfection*, edited by Thomas H. Bestul (2000)

John Lydgate, *The Siege of Thebes*, edited by Robert R. Edwards (2001)

Pearl, edited by Sarah Stanbury (2001)

The Trials and Joys of Marriage, edited by Eve Salisbury (2002)

Middle English Legends of Women Saints, edited by Sherry L. Reames, with the assistance of Martha G. Blalock and Wendy R. Larson (2003)

The Wallace: Selections, edited by Anne McKim (2003)

Richard Maidstone, *Concordia (The Reconciliation of Richard II with London)*, edited by David R. Carlson, with a verse translation by A. G. Rigg (2003)

Three Purgatory Poems: The Gast of Gy, Sir Owain, The Vision of Tundale, edited by Edward E. Foster (2004)

William Dunbar, *The Complete Works*, edited by John Conlee (2004)

Chaucerian Dream Visions and Complaints, edited by Dana M. Symons (2004)

Stanzaic Guy of Warwick, edited by Alison Wiggins (2004)

Saints' Lives in Middle English Collections, edited by E. Gordon Whatley, with Anne B. Thompson and Robert K. Upchurch (2004)

Siege of Jerusalem, edited by Michael Livingston (2004)

The Kingis Quair and Other Prison Poems, edited by Linne R. Mooney and Mary-Jo Arn (2005)

The Chaucerian Apocrypha: A Selection, edited by Kathleen Forni (2005)

John Gower, *The Minor Latin Works*, edited and translated by R. F. Yeager, with *In Praise of Peace*, edited by Michael Livingston (2005)

Sentimental and Humorous Romances: Floris and Blancheflour, Sir Degrevant, The Squire of Low Degree, The Tournament of Tottenham, and The Feast of Tottenham, edited by Erik Kooper (2006)

The Dicts and Sayings of the Philosophers, edited by John William Sutton (2006)

Everyman and Its Dutch Original, Elckerlijc, edited by Clifford Davidson, Martin W. Walsh, and Ton J. Broos (2007)

The N-Town Plays, edited by Douglas Sugano, with assistance by Victor I. Scherb (2007)

The Book of John Mandeville, edited by Tamarah Kohanski and C. David Benson (2007)

John Lydgate, *The Temple of Glas*, edited by J. Allan Mitchell (2007)

The Northern Homily Cycle, edited by Anne B. Thompson (2008)

Codex Ashmole 61: A Compilation of Popular Middle English Verse, edited by George Shuffelton (2008)

Chaucer and the Poems of "Ch," edited by James I. Wimsatt (revised edition 2009)

William Caxton, *The Game and Playe of the Chesse*, edited by Jenny Adams (2009)

John the Blind Audelay, *Poems and Carols*, edited by Susanna Fein (2009)

Two Moral Interludes: The Pride of Life and Wisdom, edited by David Klausner (2009)

John Lydgate, *Mummings and Entertainments*, edited by Claire Sponsler (2010)

Mankind, edited by Kathleen M. Ashley and Gerard NeCastro (2010)

The Castle of Perseverance, edited by David N. Klausner (2010)

Robert Henryson, *The Complete Works*, edited by David J. Parkinson (2010)

John Gower, *The French Balades*, edited and translated by R. F. Yeager (2011)

The Middle English Metrical Paraphrase of the Old Testament, edited by Michael Livingston (2011)

The York Corpus Christi Plays, edited by Clifford Davidson (2011)

Prik of Conscience, edited by James H. Morey (2012)

The Dialogue of Solomon and Marcolf: A Dual-Language Edition from Latin and Middle English Printed Editions, edited by Nancy Mason Bradbury and Scott Bradbury (2012)

Croxton Play of the Sacrament, edited by John T. Sebastian (2012)

Ten Bourdes, edited by Melissa M. Furrow (2013)

Lybeaus Desconus, edited by Eve Salisbury and James Weldon (2013)

The Complete Harley 2253 Manuscript, Vol. 2, edited and translated by Susanna Fein with David Raybin and Jan Ziolkowski (2014); Vol. 3 (2015); Vol. 1 (2015)

Oton de Granson Poems, edited and translated by Peter Nicholson and Joan Grenier-Winther (2015)

COMMENTARY SERIES

Haimo of Auxerre, *Commentary on the Book of Jonah*, translated with an introduction and notes by Deborah Everhart (1993)

Medieval Exegesis in Translation: Commentaries on the Book of Ruth, translated with an introduction and notes by Lesley Smith (1996)

Nicholas of Lyra's Apocalypse Commentary, translated with an introduction and notes by Philip D. W. Krey (1997)

Rabbi Ezra Ben Solomon of Gerona, *Commentary on the Song of Songs and Other Kabbalistic Commentaries*, selected, translated, and annotated by Seth Brody (1999)

John Wyclif, *On the Truth of Holy Scripture*, translated with an introduction and notes by Ian Christopher Levy (2001)

Second Thessalonians: Two Early Medieval Apocalyptic Commentaries, introduced and translated by Steven R. Cartwright and Kevin L. Hughes (2001)

The "Glossa Ordinaria" on the Song of Songs, translated with an introduction and notes by Mary Dove (2004)

The Seven Seals of the Apocalypse: Medieval Texts in Translation, translated with an introduction and notes by Francis X. Gumerlock (2009)

The "Glossa Ordinaria" on Romans, translated with an introduction and notes by Michael Scott Woodward (2011)

🖋 Documents of Practice Series

Love and Marriage in Late Medieval London, selected, translated, and introduced by Shannon McSheffrey (1995)

Sources for the History of Medicine in Late Medieval England, selected, introduced, and translated by Carole Rawcliffe (1995)

A Slice of Life: Selected Documents of Medieval English Peasant Experience, edited, translated, and with an introduction by Edwin Brezette DeWindt (1996)

Regular Life: Monastic, Canonical, and Mendicant "Rules," selected and introduced by Douglas J. McMillan and Kathryn Smith Fladenmuller (1997); second edition, selected and introduced by Daniel Marcel La Corte and Douglas J. McMillan (2004)

Women and Monasticism in Medieval Europe: Sisters and Patrons of the Cistercian Reform, selected, translated, and with an introduction by Constance H. Berman (2002)

Medieval Notaries and Their Acts: The 1327–1328 Register of Jean Holanie, introduced, edited, and translated by Kathryn L. Reyerson and Debra A. Salata (2004)

John Stone's Chronicle: Christ Church Priory, Canterbury, 1417–1472, selected, translated, and introduced by Meriel Connor (2010)

🖋 Medieval German Texts in Bilingual Editions Series

Sovereignty and Salvation in the Vernacular, 1050–1150, introduction, translations, and notes by James A. Schultz (2000)

Ava's New Testament Narratives: "When the Old Law Passed Away," introduction, translation, and notes by James A. Rushing, Jr. (2003)

History as Literature: German World Chronicles of the Thirteenth Century in Verse, introduction, translation, and notes by R. Graeme Dunphy (2003)

Thomasin von Zirclaria, *Der Welsche Gast (The Italian Guest),* translated by Marion Gibbs and Winder McConnell (2009)

Ladies, Whores, and Holy Women: A Sourcebook in Courtly, Religious, and Urban Cultures of Late Medieval Germany, introductions, translations, and notes by Ann Marie Rasmussen and Sarah Westphal-Wihl (2010)

🖋 Varia

The Study of Chivalry: Resources and Approaches, edited by Howell Chickering and Thomas H. Seiler (1988)

Studies in the Harley Manuscript: The Scribes, Contents, and Social Contexts of British Library MS Harley 2253, edited by Susanna Fein (2000)

The Liturgy of the Medieval Church, edited by Thomas J. Heffernan and E. Ann Matter (2001; second edition 2005)

Johannes de Grocheio, *Ars musice,* edited and translated by Constant J. Mews, John N. Crossley, Catherine Jeffreys, Leigh McKinnon, and Carol J. Williams (2011)

🖋 To Order Please Contact:

Medieval Institute Publications
Western Michigan University
Kalamazoo, MI 49008-5432
Phone (269) 387-8755
FAX (269) 387-8750
http://www.wmich.edu/medieval/mip/index.html

Typeset in 10/13 New Baskerville
and Golden Cockerel Ornaments display

Medieval Institute Publications
College of Arts and Sciences
Western Michigan University
1903 W. Michigan Avenue
Kalamazoo, MI 49008-5432
http://www.wmich.edu/medievalpublications

 WESTERN MICHIGAN UNIVERSITY